IMAGES
of America

HISTORIC
GEORGETOWN
A WALKING TOUR

A Tour Vehicle.

IMAGES
of America

HISTORIC
GEORGETOWN
A WALKING TOUR

Thomas J. Carrier

ARCADIA
PUBLISHING

GEORGETOWN, 1850.

CONTENTS

ACKNOWLEDGMENTS

Thank you to the following for their generous support and encouragement: Mary Tiernes and Matthew Gilmore of the Washingtoniana Division of the Martin Luther King Public Library; Keith Melder, chairman emeritus of the Division of Social History of the National Museum of American History; Natalie and Edward Hughes of the Bookhouse (www.bookhouse.com) for the use of their collection as my personal library; and Christine Riley, my editor at Arcadia Publishing for her great patience and continuous support.

Special thanks go to the following: Arlene Bournia, a true friend; Renee del Solar, for her bright and cheerful support and for the use of her camera for "one week;" to Inés, for her loving support and encouragement; and, most importantly, to my Ma and Dad, who keep me grounded.

About the author: Tom Carrier has been a licensed tour guide in Washington, D.C., since 1995 although he has given unofficial tours since he visited the area while stationed at Fort Bragg, North Carolina, in the late 1970s. He has also written *The Historic Walking Tour of Alexandria 1749* and *Washington, D.C.: A Historical Walking Tour* for the *Images of America Series* from Arcadia Publishing. He has given specialized tours to the curator and the Secret Service at the White House and was a costumed interpreter for the National Park Service.

Please direct all comments on this work to the publisher. I would love to hear from you.

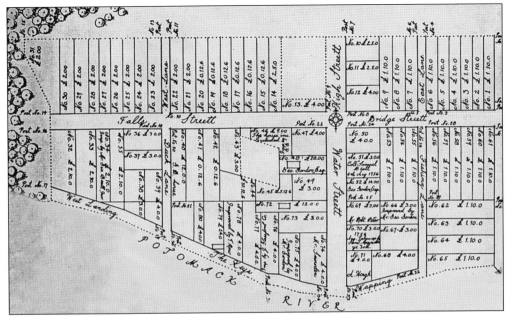

AN EARLY MAP.

INTRODUCTION

" . . . this place is without question the most pleasant in all this country
and most convenient for habitation . . ."
—Henry Fleete describing Georgetown in 1634

The Algonquin Indian Nation settled in the area well before the first visit by Captain James Cook in 1608. The village of reported Tahoga was the home of the Nacotchankes, or Anacostian, tribe, which had scattered villages all along this part of the Potomac River. This village was a central meeting place for nearly 40 Indian tribes between the Atlantic Ocean and the Potomac River, according to Thomas Jefferson.

It was inevitable that the very rivers that served the Indian Nations so well would also be used to attract the first European settlers to the region. The Royal Colony of Maryland, named for Queen Henrietta Mary of England, wife of Charles I, was created in June 1632 as a grant to Cecelius Calvert, known as the second Lord Baron of Baltimore. As a proprietor, the land was his to give or sell as he wished.

The first grant went to Col. Ninian Beall. Fighting against Cromwell as an officer of the Scottish-English Army, Beall was taken prisoner in 1650 and exiled to the West Indies. He was sent to the Colony of Maryland to complete his sentence after which he claimed several hundred acres of land from Lord Baltimore. Beall's land grant east of Rock Creek would be renamed the Rock of Dunbarton. Beall's son George inherited these acres upon his father's death in 1717 at his home in Upper Marlboro, Maryland.

The second original landowner of Georgetown was George Gordon. He was also born and raised in Scotland but, unlike Ninian Beall, was in manufacturing, not the military. Still, he was appointed sheriff of Frederick County and a judge of the first county court.

He invested in 100 acres of land known as "Knaves' Disappointment," a part of the tract that would become Georgetown.

In 1751, the Assembly of the Province of Maryland appointed commissioners to lay out a town in the County of Frederick. The boundaries of this new town of George would approximate present-day Thirty-fourth Street on the west to just below N Street on the north with Thirtieth Street on the east and the Potomac bordering the south. These are also approximately the boundaries for your tour today. The town was probably named George in order to induce George Gordon and George Beall to donate the land, or, more likely, it was named for King George III of England. Either way, the town was not named for George Washington, a 20-year-old surveyor at the time.

In 1791, George Washington included Georgetown in the new Federal City to be built across Rock Creek and occupied by the new government in 1800. The area's ready port facilities provided easy access to the building sites of the new national capital. The Chesapeake & Ohio (C&O) canal was completed through Georgetown in the 1830s, but steam navigation quickly made these canals obsolete. Still, the very successful traders were building their magnificent residences above Georgetown at a rapid rate, marking this small tobacco port as a key regional commercial center.

By 1860, a merger of the City of Washington and Georgetown was being considered but the Civil War intervened. It was finally settled in 1871, when Washington, D.C., which would now include Georgetown, would become a territory overseen by the United States Congress. (A delegate to Congress has been elected since 1974, but without the privilege of voting on legislation.)

World War II brought an increasing number of new residents to Washington, D.C., which helped transform the sleepy southern town. Space was at a premium and Georgetown neighborhoods, in decline, were alive once again. Commercial development had taken hold along the waterfront. Flour mills, warehouses, and other heavy industry dominated the area. It seemed that Georgetown's historic past would disappear, but the Old Georgetown Act of 1950 was passed and kept commercial developments from consuming its historic neighborhoods. By 1967, Georgetown was declared a National Historic Landmark. Its neighborhoods and

CIVIL WAR UNION SOLDIERS ON MASON ISLAND, C. 1861, ACROSS FROM THE GEORGETOWN WATERFRONT.

WATERFRONT, 1968.

waterfront areas grew, once again, to be a fashionable place to live, visit, shop, and relax. Its 18th- and 19th-century charms have been preserved in its architecture, cobblestone streets, historic homes, and neighborhood businesses.

Unfortunately, this limited format does not allow a complete look at Georgetown's historic past. Mostly, sites were included that served to tell its story through an available photograph or image. On occasion, though, a site was important enough to include even though an image was unavailable. In certain cases, you will find that a site may have a slightly different historic interpretation. Although my resources are as recent and varied as possible, new or additional information may have been uncovered since the publication of this book. Still, all errors or perpetuation of historic myth are unintentional and are my responsibility.

All in all, there are over 200 images and over 160 sites covered here—more than any other walking tour in print today. The book's layout is designed for you to take each tour separately and they are expected to last no more than 1.5 to 2 hours. Naturally, you should end your tour close to where you started, which will make it easier to find your way home again. Of course, I have made it easy to combine tours by creating a site that "links" other tours as you walk. It all depends on your own energy. Occasionally, you will hear recollections from Christian Hines, who lived virtually his whole life in Washington, D.C., from a young teenager in 1796 until his death in 1875 at the age of 94; he lived through the changes from woodland to world capital.

Most restaurants, shopping, restrooms, telephones, and ATMs are located in and around the waterfront and Wisconsin Avenue. As you continue northward through the neighborhoods, a corner store is usually the place to stop for things to eat and drink. Restrooms will be found in visitor areas such as Dunbarton Oaks, Georgetown Library, and Montrose Park, otherwise they can be rather scarce. For those with special needs such as wheelchairs, remember that this is a 19th-century neighborhood and getting around will not always be easy, but it is possible. Prepare any special needs beforehand.

One last piece of advice. As you walk the alleyways, streets, and gardens, remember to look up. You just might discover more history.

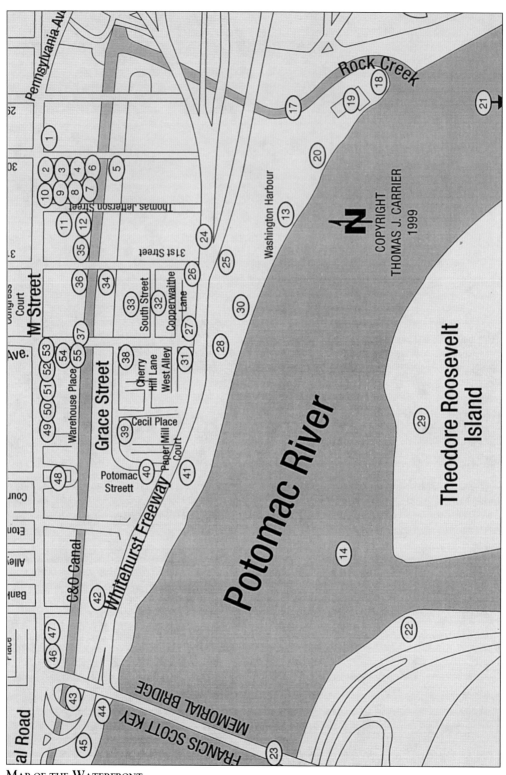

MAP OF THE WATERFRONT.

Tour A

THE WATERFRONT

If you look at the Georgetown waterfront from Analostan Island (Theodore Roosevelt Island today) in the 1860s and compare it to the waterfront today, the differences would be striking. Then, warehouses of all types were crowded along what is now K Street. Today, very little is left except the Whitehurst Freeway and a large parking lot that is soon to be Waterfront Park managed by the National Park Service.

In short, this area from N Street south to the Potomac River was one of the most important commercial and shipping ports in the world and helped provide food, clothing, wood, and other essentials for families along the Chesapeake Bay, the Potomac River, and for other colonies and states to the west. The area's importance helped settle the question as to where to locate the national capital of an expanding nation.

There is much to see here. Many original buildings of early Georgetown remain, such as the home of the first mayor of Georgetown, Robert Peter, on South Street. The C&O Canal still wends its way through Georgetown just as it has since 1828 but only because it was saved from destruction in 1954. Georgetown's rapid rise in the 17th and 18th centuries to its slow economic decline after the Civil War and into the early 20th century allowed many historic buildings to be demolished in the name of progress. But in 1950, the Old Georgetown Act that renewed the effort to "preserve and protect the places and areas of historic interest" in Georgetown was passed. This helps maintain the historic character of Georgetown today.

We'll begin our tour of the waterfront by visiting one of the many churches that existed here, this one built through a contribution of one of the earliest, most prominent Georgetown residents.

SITE A1: BRIDGE STREET PRESBYTERIAN CHURCH ON THE SOUTHEAST CORNER OF M AND THIRTIETH STREETS. A small, red brick church occupied this site as early as 1781, and the Secretary of State Thomas Jefferson was an original subscriber. In 1801, the church was enlarged. In 1821, a new church was built, but it was razed in 1871. The founder of the church, Rev. Stephen Bloomer Balch, also taught at Georgetown College (Site C1). He drilled his classes in military maneuvers and then commanded them during the Battle of Bladensburg in 1814. Balch remained pastor for 53 years and is buried at Oak Hill Cemetery (Site E12). The congregation moved to the West Street Presbyterian Church (Site F27) by 1873.

SITE A2: JOHN MOUNTZ HOMES AT 3012/3016 M STREET (LATHAM HOTEL SITE). On the Latham Hotel Site stood two distinctive homes. The first was the home of John Abbott, a schoolteacher, whose father moved from Philadelphia with the transfer of government to the new Federal City in 1800. The second home belonged to John Mountz, the first Clerk of the Corporation of the city of George Town when it was incorporated in 1789, a position Mountz held until 1856 (for 67 years)!

SITE A3: MCLEERY HOUSE AT 1068 THIRTIETH STREET. This Federal-style brick house and land that included a 2-foot alley were obtained by Henry McCleery in 1801 from Thomas Beall for about $2,000. It is thought that the house may have been designed by James Hoban, the architect of the White House, as early as 1800, making this one of the oldest houses in Georgetown. Like many houses in this area, the street was raised when the Chesapeake & Ohio Canal was built, and therefore, the original first floor is now below street level.

TIE ROD STAR. As you walk around Georgetown, even in this neighborhood, look more closely at the sides of early houses and buildings. Until about the Civil War, many structures were held together with a cast-iron pole through each end of the building. Each end was secured using a cast-iron tie rod usually cast as a decorative star. This helped to maintain the integrity of structures that were more than one story tall.

13

SITE A4: McGowan and Shinn Rowhouses at 1058–1066 Thirtieth Street. These Victorian-style rowhouses, built about 1887, are named for their original owners. The houses have been altered from their original Victorian style in an attempt to create a more colonial appearance, but this attempt has not succeeded architecturally. For example, the doors originally had rectangular transoms and wooden lintels similar to those over the windows. As you walk through Georgetown there are many similar rowhouses, such as Wheatley Row on Twenty-ninth Street, built during the same period.

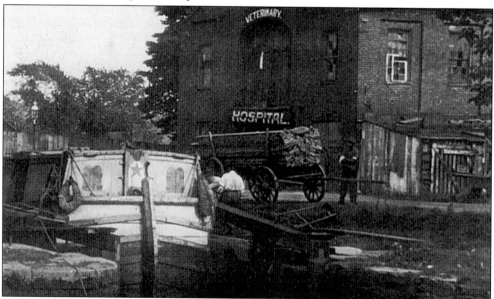

SITE A5: The Duvall Foundry at 1050 Thirtieth Street. With easy access to the C&O Canal, rail, river, and land transportation, this foundry, built in 1856 by William Duvall, forged much-needed tools and other implements during the Civil War. Following the war, the foundry was no longer as vital, and it was renovated and used as a veterinary hospital, a stable, a stonecutter's shop, and artists' studios. With extensive renovation, the structure was reopened as a restaurant and the principal building of The Foundry shopping mall in 1976.

Site A6: The Chesapeake and Ohio Canal Lock #3 at Tow Path and Thirtieth Street.
This is one of the few locks that still survives as part of the C&O Canal. When completed in 1852, the canal stretched 186 miles from Georgetown to Cumberland, Maryland, descending 578 feet. Begun as a speculative development to link the Ohio River with eastern seaports, the C&O Canal broke ground in 1829 on the Fourth of July with great fanfare. Even Pres. John Quincy Adams lent a hand and helped to break ground. Unfortunately, the money did not follow, and the canal was never completed to the Ohio River. By 1924, the canal was obsolete as the railroad became the cheaper form of transportation. This photo of Lock #3 was taken about 1930.

The C&O Canal. During the summer months, the canal relives its historic past when National Park Rangers in period costumes invite passengers to travel with them on an authentic canal barge pulled by mules. It is a great treat and shouldn't be missed. Tickets are available inside The Foundry Shops at the National Park Information Desk.

SITE A7: WILLIAM O. DOUGLAS STATUE AT TOW PATH AND THIRTIETH STREET. In the 1940s, Justice of the U.S. Supreme Court William O. Douglas, an avid walker, successfully crusaded to save the Georgetown portion of the C&O Canal from being filled in. Douglas's memorial can be seen in the central portion of Canal Square. Justice Douglas was born in Minnesota in 1898, became a professor of law at Yale in 1928, and was appointed chairman of the new Securities and Exchange Commission in 1937. Pres. Franklin Roosevelt appointed him associated justice to the Supreme Court in 1939 where he served until 1975. Douglas died in 1980.

JUSTICE WILLIAM O. DOUGLAS (CENTER) ON ONE OF HIS YEARLY WALKS ALONG THE C&O TOW PATH, C. 1957. Through his efforts, the C&O Canal was named a national historic park in 1971.

SITE A8: FEDERAL HOUSE AT 1063 THOMAS JEFFERSON STREET.

Thomas Jefferson Street was laid out in 1797 on land originally owned by Robert Peter, later Georgetown's first mayor. This two-story, Federal-style residence is very similar to many homes you will see in this part of Georgetown. The stone lintels using the keystone elements throughout are one of the finest architectural touches and reminiscent of a true Federal-style home. The brick is inlaid with Flemish bond, typical of building patterns of the 18th and early 19th centuries.

SITE A9: NICHOLAS HEDGES HOUSE AT 1069 THOMAS JEFFERSON STREET.

Here is an unusual Federal-style house built on a lot also owned by Robert Peter. After Peter's death, his brother sold the lot in 1813 to Nicholas Hedges, who built this brick house sometime between 1815 and 1818. It's unusual in that the house facing the street had two doorways, one leading to the shop on the first floor and the other to the residence on the upper two floors. The shop door, originally to the left of the existing door, was bricked up during renovations in 1941.

SITE A10: BIRCH FUNERAL HOME AND STABLE AT 1083 THOMAS JEFFERSON STREET. This is a stable and garage used as part of the original Birch Funeral Home located at 3034 M Street. It is considered to be the only late-19th-century structure of its kind left in the Georgetown waterfront area. Joseph Birch was an undertaker and cabinetmaker when he bought the property in 1857 for $1,600. The present buildings were erected sometime between 1866 and 1871. Joseph F. Birch's Sons, funeral directors, operated here until 1965. According to a local historian, the Birch Funeral Home handled all of the burials in Arlington and Alexandria during its earlier years when these localities did not have their own funeral parlors. By 1891, Joseph Birch had died leaving his sons George and Isaac the business. It remained in the family until the property was sold in 1966. The storefront on M Street retains some of its 19th-century embellishments to this day.

THE OLD BIRCH FUNERAL HOME, 3034 M STREET, C. 1965.

SITE A11: ADAMS-MASON HOUSE AT 1072 THOMAS JEFFERSON STREET. Thomas Adams bought this section of Robert Peter's property in 1808 and erected this wooden-frame, Federal-style house before selling the property in 1812. George W. Mason, a carriage maker, bought this house and lot and the one next door at 1074 about 1880, and subsequent generations of his family occupied the house until 1964. It is believed that the structure between these two houses originally served the George Mason as a stable and carriage workshop.

SITE A12: THE POTOMAC MASONS LODGE #5 AT 1058 THOMAS JEFFERSON STREET. Lodge 43 of the Masons had its original headquarters in a private home farther down Jefferson Street, and it was from that site that members participated alongside George Washington in the laying of the cornerstone at the Capitol on September 18, 1793. The Mason's new headquarters was built here in 1810 and was occupied by the group until 1840. Later, the Gormley family operated a grocery and china store here until about 1940. The site has been used as offices, a bank, and a private home since then.

SITE A13: WASHINGTON HARBOUR (KNOWN AS HARBOR PLACE) AT 3000 K STREET. In 1986, this huge complex of shops, offices, and condominiums was created by Arthur Cotton Moore. The American Institute of Architects' *Guide to the Architecture of Washington, D.C.* quotes Moore as saying that his use of columns, domes, and seemingly different architectural styles "reflects . . . the exuberant three-dimensional vocabulary of Victorian Georgetown in an abstract way." The style is definitely reminiscent of Jeffersonian and Federal styles. Visit for awhile. The next couple of pages will point out the sights you see from the docks of Washington Harbour.

SITE A14: POTOMAC RIVER. Actually, this is the Georgetown Channel. It runs along Theodore Roosevelt Island (in front of you). Just south of the island (to your left) is the Potomac River. In 1790, Arlington, Virginia, and Alexandria, Virginia, were a part of Washington, D.C., and, during the Civil War, provided forts for the defense of the capital. In 1848, the federal government returned these communities to Virginia, but the Potomac River remains within the territory of Washington, D.C. Now, let's identify other landmarks beginning to your left.

SITE A15: THE WATERGATE COMPLEX AT 2650 VIRGINIA AVENUE, NW. The Watergate was a project developed by the Societa Generale Immobiliare (SGI) and was completed in 1971. On June 17, 1972, security guard Frank Wills removed tape over a basement door lock, and two years later, Pres. Richard Nixon resigned for trying to cover-up the burglary of the Democratic National Committee headquarters. A plaque on the sixth floor commemorates this historical event. Across the street at 2601 Virginia Avenue is the former Howard Johnson Motor Hotel (now student housing for George Washington University). In room 723, other "plumbers" watched for police prior to the break-in.

SITE A16: THE JOHN F. KENNEDY CENTER FOR THE PERFORMING ARTS AT 2700 F STREET, NW. In 1971 after 12 years of planning and construction, this new national cultural center designed by Edward Durrell Stone was completed and named as a memorial to the assassinated 35th President of the United States. The infamous "Deep Throat" met with reporters Woodward and Bernstein in the underground parking garage here during their investigation of the Watergate break-in. Nearby is Braddock's Landing where legend says Gen. Edward Braddock stepped ashore with his aide Lt. Col. George Washington on his way to fight in the French and Indian War at Fort Duquesne near Pittsburgh in 1755. The Christian Heurich Brewery stood here from 1892 to 1961, producing 10,000 barrels of beer in its heyday.

SITE A17: ROCK CREEK. As a tributary of the Potomac River, Rock Creek essentially separated the City of Washington (or Territory of Columbia as it was officially known) and the port of Georgetown. Rock Creek connects West Potomac Park near the Franklin Roosevelt Memorial with the National Zoo. Rock Creek is part of Rock Creek Park, 1,800 acres of woodland set aside by Congress in 1890 as a "pleasuring ground for the benefit and enjoyment of the people of the United States."

SITE A18: CHESAPEAKE & OHIO CANAL MILE 0. Near here is the very first lock for the C&O Canal. Where you are standing is the beginning of 186 miles of canal created from Georgetown to Cumberland, Maryland. Beginning in 1829, there were a total of 74 locks built at a cost of $23 million. The canal descended a total of 578 feet from Cumberland to this point, a confluence of Rock Creek and the Potomac River.

SITE A19: THOMPSON'S BOATHOUSE. Here is a modern-style boathouse that complements the private, Victorian-style Washington Canoe Club located at the far end of Water Street in Georgetown (Site A44). The boathouse was built in the 1960s by the National Park Service for use by the rowing clubs of Georgetown University and to provide public access to the Potomac River. Gary Scott, National Park Service historian, believes the building was named for Harry T. Thompson, National Park Service regional director of that period.

SITE A20: SUN DIAL AT WASHINGTON HARBOUR. It was very difficult getting historical information about the placement of this oversized sundial. The designer was probably Arthur Cotton Moore, the architect of the Washington Harbour complex. A 16th-century invention, the sundial tells the time of day by the shadow of the gnomon (the raised metal piece) as it reflects the sun.

SITE A21: THEODORE ROOSEVELT MEMORIAL BRIDGE. This bridge connects Washington, D.C., and Northern Virginia just south of Theodore Roosevelt Island, now a nature preserve. Alice Roosevelt Longworth, Pres. Theodore Roosevelt's daughter, ceremoniously opened the bridge in 1964.

SITE A22: ROSSLYN IN ARLINGTON, VIRGINIA. Directly across the Potomac River is the skyline for Rosslyn, a neighborhood of Arlington. As one of the smallest counties in the United States, with a population of 185,000, there are no separate towns or cities in Arlington, only neighborhoods. Rosslyn was an area best described as "the red light district" of bars, pawn shops, and commercial industry until the 1950s. Today, Rosslyn is now a "concrete canyon" of mostly office buildings. The two tall, rounded towers are the headquarters for Gannett Co. and *USA Today* newspaper. Visit the Newseum, an interactive museum dedicated to the newspaper industry, located near the Rosslyn Metro station.

SITE A23: FRANCIS SCOTT KEY MEMORIAL BRIDGE. Nearby stood the home of Francis Scott Key, a lawyer and the author of the United States National Anthem. The flag that inspired Key's writing of the "Star Spangled Banner" is displayed in the American History Museum. In 1923, the bridge bearing his name replaced the aging Aqueduct Bridge that had been in place since 1833. The Francis Scott Key Memorial Bridge was designed and erected by Col. W.L. Fiske of the U.S. Army Corps of Engineers. Made of reinforced concrete, the span is 1,650 feet long and has arches within arches, "giving lightness and strength to the structure." The bridge connects Washington, D.C., with Arlington County and the western suburbs.

THE POTOMAC AQUEDUCT WITH ORIGINAL SUPERSTRUCTURE, C. 1865.

SITE A24: WHITEHURST FREEWAY. Built as an exit off the Key Bridge, the freeway is under construction in the center of this photo near the waterfront. See the waterfront development at the time and the old Aqueduct Bridge pylons still in the Potomac below the Key Bridge. Notice the Capital Traction Powerhouse (the buildings with two chimneys on the waterfront).

SITE A25: CAPITAL TRACTION CO. POWERHOUSE, FORMERLY AT 3142 K STREET (NOW A PARKING LOT). In 1818, Richard Parrott was listed as the owner of the deed to this property (Site E7) that was possibly intended for his rope making business. Prior to that, Henry Foxall (Site G14) owned the western part of the lot beginning in 1808. The Dodge brothers are also listed as owners as early as 1852 (Sites A31, F11, F14). By 1910, the site became the electrical plant that powered the streetcars that ran through Washington and the suburbs until 1967. The power plant, however, was only used until 1943 when it was abandoned; it was razed in 1968 for the Whitehurst Freeway.

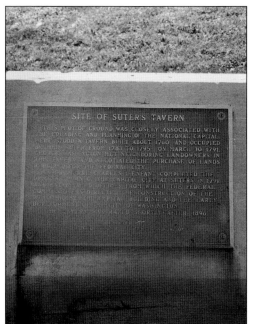

SITE A26: SUTER'S TAVERN SITE. When the photo at left was taken in June 1999, there was a plaque just inside the fence identifying this site as Suter's Tavern. It was at Suter's that George Washington signed the deed creating the Federal City, that the first commissioners met, and that Pierre L'Enfant made his headquarters. However, Christian Hines locates Suter's above the canal on Wisconsin Avenue (Site A37). Neither site has been positively identified as the location of Suter's Tavern. However, this site (at right), incorporating the old D.C. incinerator built in 1932 but abandoned by the city in 1971, will undergo a transformation as part of the Ritz Carlton hotel complex to be completed by 2001. A small historical display is supposed to replace the simple plaque. Look for it then.

SITE A27: K STREET FLOOD. This happened a lot along here. This photo was taken on October 17, 1942, and shows all of Water Street (now K Street) under severe flooding.

SITE A28: POTOMAC RIVERFRONT. This is an early image of the Georgetown waterfront along the Potomac. At this point before the Revolutionary War, a ferry operating between Maryland (Georgetown was part of Frederick County, Maryland until 1790) and Virginia consisted of an iron chain erected across the Potomac River to Analoston Island. Passengers simply pulled themselves hand over hand along the chain until they reached shore. Today, the Key Bridge, the Theodore Roosevelt Bridge, and others fulfill the same purpose.

SITE A29: THEODORE ROOSEVELT ISLAND. Known by many names—My Lord's, Barbados, Mason's, Analostan or Anacostan—this island was on the rent rolls of Lord Baltimore and was probably designated as farmland because the island was bare of trees. The island was deeded to George Mason, the writer of the Virginia State Constitution and the U.S. Bill of Rights, in 1777 and was known as Masons Island. In 1780, Col. John Mason, son of George Mason, built "the finest house in America" here, but it has long since been razed. In the 1930s, the Civilian Conservation Corps cleared most of the island and prepared it for the construction of a park named for Theodore Roosevelt that was accessible by a foot bridge off the George Washington Parkway in Virginia.

FERRY OPERATING FROM ANALOSTAN ISLAND TO GEORGETOWN, C. 1862.

SITE A30: GORDON'S WAREHOUSE. You'll just have to imagine that in this area on the river's edge just east of the foot of Wisconsin Avenue was George Gordon's Warehouse and Inspection Station. There is no image available at the time of this publication. It was the presence of this tobacco warehouse that drew trade into the area and helped establish the Town of George in 1751. Gordon was an original patentee of Georgetown and built this log house on "Conjurer's Disappointment" in 1730. It quickly became the only real place for the inspection and sorting of tobacco for miles around. George Gordon, himself, lived nearby at about 3206 M Street.

SITE A31: THE OLD DODGE WAREHOUSE AT 1000 WISCONSIN AVENUE. Considered to be one of the finest examples of architecture on the Georgetown waterfront, this warehouse was built in 1800 by two merchant brothers, Ebenezer and Francis Dodge. After the death of Francis in 1851, the brothers' two sons continued the long tradition of Georgetown's preeminence in international commerce by trading with the West Indies. However, in 1857, the brothers were bankrupt and so ended Georgetown's trade within the international community. This photo was taken *c.* 1968 by the National Park Service.

Site A32: Robert Peter Home at 3134–36 South Street. This was the home of the first mayor of Georgetown, Robert Peter, in 1789. Originally from Scotland, Peter arrived in George Town and quickly became a wealthy tobacco merchant and landholder. His son married Martha Parke Custis, a granddaughter of Martha Washington. The family home was moved in July 1999 to undergo restoration but will return to this site by 2001 as part of the new Ritz Carlton hotel complex.

Site A33: Grace Episcopal Church at 1041 Wisconsin Avenue. The church building was a small frame chapel when it was constructed on "Brickyard Hill" in 1855. In 1867, this new church was built for a cost of $25,000. The church was known for catering to the seamen whose docks were nearby and to the bargemen making their way up the C&O Canal.

SITE A34: 1038 THIRTY-FIRST STREET. This is just an example of some of the early Federal-style townhouses that have become prevalent in Georgetown since the Civil War. You notice that the houses appear to sit on a high ridge, but when the C&O Canal was being dug, the grading of the streets was changed. In many instances, you will need to look up to view some of the architectural and historical detail of many Georgetown sites.

CANAL COMPANY HOUSE AT 1061 THIRTY-FIRST STREET. Brick is an excellent example of early commercial architecture devoted to the C&O Canal. Here, a small, two-story building built in 1830 served the original C&O Canal Co. as storage space. Sometime later, the structure became a tavern and then a stable to house the mules that pulled barges through the canal (the drivers lived upstairs). In 1941, the house was renovated as apartments and is still used as such today. The only changes to the structure seem to be the addition of two doors on the first floor and the three apartments carved inside where there were once only two.

SITE A36: HOLLERITH BUILDING AT 1058 THIRTY-FIRST STREET. In this building, Herman Hollerith perfected a punch-card tabulating machine and created a company to manufacture it. His invention was used in tabulating the U.S. census of 1890 and 1900. He operated his company, Tabulating Machine Co., from this building from 1892 until 1911 when he sold the business to the Computing-Tabulating-Recording Co., which later became International Business Machine Co. in 1924 and is known today simply as IBM. IBM continued operating at this location until about World War II. The building now houses several business offices. Hollerith died in 1929 at the age of 69.

SITE A37: SUTER'S TAVERN #2 (FOUNTAIN INN). Is this the site where Robert Peter built a one-story, frame building about 1761 and leased it to John Suter for the operation of what was to be known as Suter's Tavern? Christian Hines says, "The election between Mr. Jefferson and Mr. Adams . . . was held in Suter's tavern . . . in 1800. The house was a one story frame, and stood on High [Wisconsin Ave.] street, between Bridge [M St.] and Water [K St.] streets, and a little east of the canal bridge." What do you think?

SITE A38: OLD WOODEN BUILDING ON THE NORTHEAST CORNER OF WISCONSIN AVENUE AND GRACE STREET. This building didn't come with a name or a history, but it was located on this spot prior to the current structure. This image was found among the many images available from the Washingtoniana Division of the D.C. Public Library. Perhaps more information about the building's original owners can be discovered later.

SITE A39: CHERRY HILL ROWHOUSES AT 1033–1043 CECIL PLACE. This area east of Potomac Street to Cecil Place was known as Cherry Hill because the original street name of Potomac Street was Cherry Street. Speculators built these simple rowhouses beginning in the middle of the 19th century in order to accommodate a rapidly growing population. The cost of a rowhouse was very economical, which explains why this entire area was filled with rowhouses built between 1870 and 1890. Each house is exactly 24 feet long and 12 feet wide, and each has a garden in the back.

SITE A40: BOMFORD MILL AT 3261 K STREET. A former flour mill was operated here by Col. George Bomford from 1832 until 1844 when it was destroyed by fire. In 1845, Bomford erected a cotton mill on the ruins of his flour mill. The new enterprise was not successful, and it was sold to Thomas Wilson of Baltimore in 1850. However, a mill has been operated on this same site in one form or another until the present day.

SITE A41: RAY'S WAREHOUSE, FORMERLY 3260 K STREET (NOW A PARKING LOT). Here, Alexander Ray operated a mill, a coal company (as agent for the Loacoming Coal and Transportation Co. of Washington), and warehouses beginning about 1823. Ray owned a great deal of waterfront property, which contributed to his commercial success until his death in 1878. He left his properties to his sons, but the lots were finally sold out of the family in 1885. The current parking lot was created in the 1970s for use by the National Park Service and may be part of a waterfront park planned for this area sometime in the early 2000s.

Site A42: Hibiscus Cafe at 3401 Water Street. This is just an example of how many older commercial buildings have been transformed into successful service industries and, in this case, a cafe. Stop in and rest a moment.

Site A43: Early Waterfront Buildings at the West End of Water Street. These photos show a very small part of the kind of commercial buildings that existed here until the 1960s. According to the National Park Service, the taller brick structure (left) was an old electrical pumping station built to provide power to the flour and other mills that once flourished here. The pumping station stopped operating in the 1920s. The smaller, one-story building (right) was probably an office. These buildings are owned by the National Park Service today, and, as you can see, even these simple commercial structures will soon disappear. A longtime resident in her early 90s remembers, around 1905, a paper mill being situated on this spot that was owned and managed by a man the children knew only as "Bunny" Smith.

SITE A44: JACK'S BOATS AT 3500 K STREET. Sons Frank and Bill run the old boathouse now, but their father, Jack Baxter, began renting boats here in 1945 when this was truly a busy waterfront. The shack itself looks old, but Bill tells me that's because its been flooded several times. Jack, a D.C. institution, died in August 1999 at the age of 86. Next door is the Potomac Boat Club, a private club that has been here since the early 20th century. Right next to the club is a pylon from the old Aqueduct Bridge that was razed in 1923 to accommodate the Key Bridge (Site A23).

SITE A45: WASHINGTON CANOE CLUB AT THE WEST END OF K STREET. Next to the Potomac Boat Club is a Shingle-style boat club, a style most prominent in resorts built for wealthy "boaters" in the late 19th century. Built in 1890, the wooden turrets on either side of the hipped roof are each three stories tall and represent this romantic style very well. The club can be seen only from the water or along the C&O Canal walking trail. Otherwise, it is a private club.

SITE A46: FRANCIS SCOTT KEY MEMORIAL SITE AT 3518 M STREET. The actual site of the home and office of the author of the "Star Spangled Banner" is now the Whitehurst Freeway exit ramp to the Key Bridge (on your right) that connects Arlington, Virginia, with Georgetown. Key lived at the house from 1805 until 1830. The house was built by Thomas Clarke in 1802 and was razed to build the ramp in 1935. The Key Bridge replaced the old Aqueduct Bridge in 1923. Stay and read the informative plaques erected by the Francis Scott Key Foundation.

FRANCIS SCOTT KEY (1779–1843). Francis Scott Key was a lawyer and sometime poet born in Frederick County, Maryland, in 1779. While trying to save a friend from captivity on a British vessel during the seize of Baltimore by invading British troops on September 13, 1814, Key was detained, too. The British bombarded Fort McHenry where Baltimore's defenses were concentrated through the night. After the smoke cleared on the morning of September 14, Key penned the words that would become the National Anthem of the United States in 1931. See the 15-star flag that inspired the song at the Museum of American History in Washington, D.C.

SITE A47: FORREST-MARBURY HOUSE AT 3350 M STREET (EMBASSY OF UKRAINE). One of the most prestigious homes in Georgetown, this house was built in 1785 by Col. Uriah Forrest, an original proprietor of the land that became the Federal City. In 1800, this house was sold to William Marbury, the first president of the Farmers and Mechanics Bank and a justice of the peace appointed by the outgoing President, John Adams. Pres. Thomas Jefferson was inaugurated before the commission could be delivered, and it was voided. Marbury sued, and the Supreme Court made a decision in *Marbury vs. Madison* that upheld Marbury's commission and the right of the Supreme Court to determine the constitutionality of laws passed by Congress.

SITE A48: BUTCHER'S MARKET AT 3276 M STREET (DEAN AND DELUCA). Butcher's Market, the earliest Georgetown market, was held on this pre-Revolutionary site, which has, since that time, always served as a market. The current building, built in the early 1800s, also served as the site for meetings of the early commissioners. The second floor has since been removed.

SITE A49: JACKSON HOUSE AT 3250 M STREET. Merchant George Walker bought this lot in 1802 and built two houses on it—one to rent and one (in the rear) to live in. In 1810, Joseph Jackson bought the two houses, set up a grocery store in one and lived in the other. Jackson's son Richard used the house facing M Street as his law office, but when he died in 1891, his wife sold both houses out of the family. The house was razed in 1906.

SITE A50: THE WAREHOUSE LOT AT 3222 M STREET (GEORGETOWN PARK MALL). In the early days of Georgetown shipping, the hogsheads of tobacco and bales of cotton were stored here. The area was known as Warehouse Lot, a temporary storage area for goods unloaded from ships docked at the waterfront. The current building was completely renovated inside in 1980 but the late 19th century facade (a repair facility for streetcars) remains.

Site A51: The Bank of Columbia at 3208 M Street. The first chartered bank in Georgetown operated here from 1793 until 1807 when it moved farther down M Street. The bank eventually failed in 1836, wiping out its depositors and stockholders. After the bank moved, this building became a hotel for a time, then Georgetown's Town Hall from 1845 through 1878 where the town's mayor and council served. In 1883, Firehouse #5 was operated from this site until 1940. Various commercial enterprises have occupied the site since.

Site A52: The City Tavern at 3206 M Street. Clement Sewell, a former employee of Suter's Tavern, built this "gentleman's" tavern in 1796. Just to the right was an entrance that served as the main terminus of the stage coach line in Georgetown. It was at this tavern, on June 16, 1800, that Pres. John Adams was given a dinner to mark his first visit to the new Federal City to inspect its development. The tavern's name was changed to the Indian King by subsequent owner Joseph Semmes in 1801 and eventually changed to the City Tavern when the establishment became a private club in 1962.

SITE A53: TOBACCO WAREHOUSES SITE. To the left, along M Street, were three large tobacco sheds, each covering 2 acres, were located here in 1791, according to well-known philanthropist W.W. Corcoran. As early as 1761, these were the only tobacco inspection houses in all of Frederick County, Maryland. An old sketch provides an example of what the barn may have looked like.

SITE A54: THE VIGILANT FIREHOUSE AT 1066 WISCONSIN AVENUE. This firehouse (now a restaurant) was built in 1844. Organized in 1817, the Vigilant volunteer firefighting brigade was the oldest firehouse in District of Columbia. Near the roof is a large "V" shaped from metal tie rods. In colonial times, homeowners subscribed to a volunteer fire brigade as you would to an insurance company. When you had a fire, your company came to put it out. Competition was fierce, which might explain the plaque at sidewalk level memorializing "Bush the Old Fire Dog," the company mascot, who was killed by poison. The photo is c. 1950.

SITE A55: THE CHESAPEAKE AND OHIO CANAL COMMEMORATIVE MARKER AT WISCONSIN AVENUE AND GEORGETOWN PARK MALL. This granite marker, measuring approximately 10 feet high and nearly 2 feet across, commemorates the dedication of the Chesapeake and Ohio Canal on October 10, 1850. The individuals that made the canal possible are listed on all four sides of the memorial, which was found abandoned in an old mill in 1889 and erected on this site in 1900 by Mr. H.P. Gilbert at his own expense. The inscriptions are the only records of the canal in existence.

THE INSPECTION STATION HOUSE AT CONSTITUTION AND SEVENTEENTH STREET. Visit the only other reminder of the C&O Canal, besides the canal itself, in Washington, D.C. This inspection house has been here since 1830 and is now a National Park Service storage building.

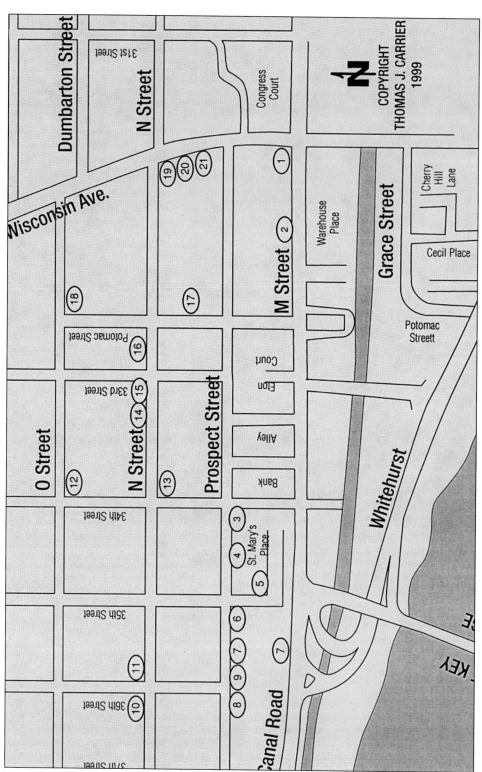

MAP OF SOUTH GEORGETOWN.

44

Tour B

SOUTHWEST
GEORGETOWN

For a time, you will still explore along M Street, or Falls Street as it was known west of Wisconsin Avenue when this area was founded in 1751. Many shops along this main avenue are virtually unchanged since then and still have the unique character of a working shop on the ground floor with offices and living space above. Only in that earlier period, the original shop owner lived here full time.

As you exit M Street and continue north, shops make way for neighborhoods where the rich and wealthy made their homes. Some did so to keep an eye on the port below while their ships were being loaded or unloaded. You will visit many of the fine mansions of the 18th and 19th centuries and meet many of the legends of early Georgetown, such as Benjamin Stoddard, John Cox, and Ambassador Alexander de Bodisco and his lovely wife. These were well-known names 150 years ago.

Then, there are the workmen, tradesmen, and other historical figures as well. William Thornton lived along M Street while fulfilling his duties as the architect of the Capitol, and the Victorian novelist E.D.E.N Southworth lived on a hill with a view of the Capitol Dome. Senator John F. Kennedy lived here before he began his presidency in 1961. You will even visit the site where an "exorcism" shook the world.

Streetcars moved through this area for just 100 years from 1860 until 1960, but the tracks are still visible. Only busses and cars run through these neighborhoods now. Georgetown University students, professors, and alumni dominate many of the antebellum townhouses. But, occasionally you might see a well-known resident, too.

Site B1: Potomac Lodge #5 at 1212 Wisconsin Avenue. The Gothic Revival facade you see in the early photo below, c. 1930, bears little resemblance to the storefront you see today. That's because a fire in the basement in 1963 virtually gutted the building, which had to be rebuilt. The Potomac Lodge of Georgetown, chartered in 1789, is the oldest lodge in Washington, D.C. It was first located at Jefferson Street and the C&O Canal (Site A12) but moved into this building in 1858.

1212 Wisconsin Avenue. When the Weaver family bought this building in 1963 (the Lodge could not rebuild), the entire facade was changed to the current Federal Revival style. The Weavers opened their general "nuts and bolts" hardware business as a storefront operation in 1989. About 1995, the storefront operation was moved to the second floor and altered its business focus to upscale fixtures. The storefront now holds an upscale clothing store.

Site B2: The Home of William Thornton at 3221 M Street.

While supervising construction as the architect of the Capitol, William Thornton lived here. Thornton was the first superintendent of patents, a post he held from 1802 until his death in 1828. George Washington was also said to have visited here. The building itself has undergone a transformation, having only two of its original three stories still in place. Thornton also designed Octagon House, Tudor Place, and George Washington's speculative townhouses located near the Capitol.

William Thornton. William Thornton won the competition for design of the Capitol in 1792 and remained as its architect until 1803 when he was replaced by Benjamin Latrobe Thornton also served as a commissioner of the District of Columbia from 1794 until 1802—not bad for a young man born Jost Van Dyke in the West Indies in 1759. He changed his name when he immigrated to the United States in 1787.

SITE B3: HALCYON HOUSE AT 3400 PROSPECT STREET. This was the home of Benjamin Stoddard, an original proprietor of the land used for the new Federal City, a cavalry major in the Continental Army who was wounded at the Battle of Brandywine, and the first U.S. secretary of the navy. This house was built in 1786 "after the manner of some of the elegant houses I have seen in Philadelphia." It obviously stands out, as you can see, with its classic pediments and an Italian gate in front of an early American doorway. Albert Clemon bought the house in 1900 and expanded the house unmercifully. It is now a series of apartments.

SITE B4: QUALITY HILL AT 3425 PROSPECT STREET. John Thompson Mason, nephew of George Mason of Gunston Hall and Analoston Island (Site A29), built this house in 1798 from brick imported from England. The house was named Quality Hill by its subsequent owner, Dr. Charles Worthington, an American physician during the War of 1812. Dr. Worthington notably attended the wounds of a British colonel who was injured during the British burning raid on the White House and the Capitol in August 1814.

SITE B5: ROCK HILL AT 11201–1211 THIRTY-FIFTH STREET. This is the neighborhood that runs along Thirty-fifth Street past Prospect Street to M Street. You might guess that the neighborhood got its name from the cobblestones in the street, and you would be right. The cobblestones are probably from ballast used in ships, but that has not been confirmed. The photo was taken about 1947.

SITE B6: PROSPECT-MORRIS HOUSE AT 3508 PROSPECT. Gen. James Lingam may have built this well-proportioned, fully restored home some time between 1788 and 1792, but it was John Templeman who originally owned this section of Georgetown and called it Pretty Prospect. A letter shows that Pres. John Adams was treated to dinner here during his first visit to the new Federal City in 1800. The house was inherited by Lt. Cmdr. George Upham Morris, whose daughter eloped with a dry goods clerk by the name of William Wilson Corcoran. Prospect House was the home of the first secretary of defense, James Forrestal, from the late 1940s until his death in 1949. This building was also used as a guest house for foreign visitors while the White House underwent extensive renovations in the 1950s.

SITE B7: CAPITAL TRACTION CO. PROSPECT STREET PAVILION IN THE 3500 BLOCK OF PROSPECT STREET. In the era when passengers traveled by way of streetcars instead of the Metro and busses, this was an important passenger station. Located just behind the Pavilion was the Thirty-sixth and M Street main headquarters of the Capital Traction Co. from 1950 to 1962, when the era of streetcars in this city ended. Washington, D.C., was the second city in the country, coming after New York City, to employ an underground electrical system to move cars throughout Washington, north to Beltsville, Maryland, and west into the suburbs. A main powerhouse was at 3142 K Street at the end of Thirty-first Street (Site A25), but it, like the streetcar, is now long gone.

MAIN HEADQUARTERS OF THE CAPITAL TRACTION CO. Located at Thirty-sixth and M Streets, from 1950 to 1962, this site now contains private offices.

SITE B8: SOUTHWORTH COTTAGE AT 3600 PROSPECT STREET. This was the site of the home of Mrs. Emma Dorothy Eliza Neville (E.D.E.N.) Southworth, a prolific novelist of the Victorian era. With a commanding view of the Potomac River, the cottage had a "Carpenters Gothic" style that was as unusual as its vantage point. Mrs. Southworth died in the house in 1899, and the cottage was razed in 1941. The two current brick townhouses were erected in 1950 and used as exterior shots in the 1973 movie *The Exorcist.*

SITE B9: *THE EXORCIST* STAIRS. The long stairs to the left of the property were also prominently featured in the film starring Linda Blair, Max von Sydow, Ellen Burstyn, and Lee J. Cobb. The story centers on the evil possession of a girl, played by a young Linda Blair. In the movie's climactic scene, the priest, played by von Sydow, allows the devil to exit the girl's body and enter his own. As its evil overwhelms him, the priest throws himself out of a window overlooking these stairs (the window was a film set; the house did not extend out this far), falls down this rather steep incline, and . . . well, have you seen the movie?

SITE B10: GEORGETOWN UNIVERSITY HOSPITAL SITE ON THE NORTHWEST CORNER OF THIRTY-SIXTH AND N STREETS. Created in 1848, the original Georgetown University Hospital was located here. The hospital was a non-sectarian facility that maintained a nurses' training school and a maternity department, established an outpatient dispensary, and housed a social service department. The original hospital closed in 1947 when the new hospital opened on campus.

SITE B11: HOLY TRINITY CHURCH AT 3525 N STREET. On the left at 3513 N Street is Holy Trinity Church, built in 1849. The original church, built in 1794, is the smaller structure found at 3525 N Street and is considered to be the first Roman Catholic church in the District of Columbia. Early religious accommodations here were so sparse that worshipers brought their own chairs for services. The first wooden pews were built by a contractor who rented them out and used the proceeds to help pay for his son's education. During the Civil War, the church served as a Union hospital. It is now the Convent of Mercy, whose sisters teach at the nearby parochial schools.

Site B12: Bodisco House at 3322 O Street. This is a former Russian Embassy and the home of Baron Alexander de Bodisco, Russian ambassador to the United States from 1837 until his death here in 1854. Built in 1815, this house was the site of any lavish social events. In 1850, at an extravagant Christmas party for his nephews, Bodisco fell in love with 16-year-old Harriet Williams, a descendant of Alexander Beall. Bodisco was 63. The two were married in May 1851, and the wedding was the most elaborate ever held in Georgetown, with Pres. Martin Van Buren, Henry Clay, and virtually the entire diplomatic corps in attendance.

Site 13: Hopkins House at 3340 N Street. It was here that Harry Hopkins made his home with his wife and daughter Diana after working with Pres. Franklin D. Roosevelt to create the New Deal. Hopkins only lived here about a year before he died.

SITE B14: COX'S ROW AT 3327–39 N STREET. John Cox was the mayor of Georgetown from 1823 through 1845 and lived at 3339 N Street during this time. These homes were built between 1815 and 1818 and are excellent examples of Federal-style architecture with their interesting, recessed festoons. At 3337, Cox entertained the Marquis de Lafayette during his visit to the United States in 1824. Apparently, there is a tunnel leading from Cox's garden to the Potomac River.

SITE B15: MARBURY-SEN. JOHN F. KENNEDY HOUSE AT 3307 N STREET. This was the home of William Marbury after he moved from M Street (Site A47) in 1812. Sen. John F. Kennedy bought this house as a present for his wife, Jacqueline, and new baby girl, Caroline. After their stay in this house, the Kennedys moved into the White House. After leaving the White House, Jacqueline Kennedy moved briefly into another N Street property (Site G11).

SITE B16: SMITH ROW AT 3255–3267 N STREET. This series of Federal-style rowhouses has the distinction of being a complete line of attached houses in an entire block. Built in 1815 by Walter and Clement Smith, these rowhouses have maintained virtually the same architectural features since then. There is a story that in widening and paving N Street in 1872, a giant sycamore planted in 1820 and standing 120 feet high stood in the way, according to Mary Mitchell in her *Georgetown Life, 1865–1900.* The tree's roots were deeply embedded under the dirt road in front of 3265 N Street, and a 19-foot-deep ditch had to be dug to remove them. It took nearly a month to remove that tree. Saving the tree might be our priority today.

SITE B17: JOSEPH CARLETON HOUSE AT 1052–1054 POTOMAC STREET. Joseph Carleton, the postmaster of Georgetown from 1799 until 1803, bought this original lot in 1794. This house was built about 1800 and is very simple in design. As with a number of homes built in Georgetown beginning in the late 18th century, this building also housed a business on the ground floor while the top two floors were occupied as private residences.

SITE B18: ST. JOHN'S CHURCH AT POTOMAC AND O STREETS. Established in 1794, this is the second oldest Episcopal church in the District of Columbia. The present church was built in 1807–1809 from plans drawn by William Thornton, the architect of the Capitol and the Octagon House (see his home at Site B2). The church has gone through extensive renovation over the years, particularly to remove the Gothic additions and restore the original Thornton design. Original subscribers included Thomas Jefferson and Dolley Madison. Enter the small Chapel of the Carpenter, fashioned entirely of rough-hewn wood, on Potomac Street for reflection and rest.

Grace Dunlop Ecker in her book *A Portrait of Old Georgetown* recounts that an old writer in 1811 wrote that " . . . the church was thronged to an overflow with all who were most elevated in station and in wealth from the Capital . . ." But the pastor had died in 1831 and the congregation could not agree on a succession. For seven years the church was virtually abandoned. There were so many bats and birds nesting in the church it was called the Swallow Barn. In fact, an artist had taken up residence in the church for a while. By 1838, the congregation had finally elected a new vestry and the church flourished once again.

SITE B19: CORCORAN STORE SITE ON THE NORTHWEST CORNER OF WISCONSIN AND N STREETS. W.W. Corcoran opened his first store on this site and began his career as a philanthropist and art collector in this "Thread and Needle" shop. He later went on to found the Corcoran Gallery of Art in 1859. Corcoran's former home stood on the site of the U.S. Chamber of Commerce at Lafayette Square, and he is buried in Oak Hill Cemetery. In the early 1800s, the Mitchell's Boys School was located on the northeast corner of this intersection.

WILLIAM WILSON CORCORAN (1798–1888), FINANCIER AND PHILANTHROPIST. Visit the Renwick Gallery on Lafayette Square in Washington, D.C., erected by Corcoran in 1859 to house his private collection of art and sculpture. Designed by James Renwick, it was instead used by the government as a hospital and headquarters for the Quartermaster Corps during the Civil War. Corcoran Gallery finally opened in 1869. Corcoran moved his collection to his new building on Seventeenth Street in 1897.

Site B20: Forrest Hall at 1262 Wisconsin Avenue. Before the Civil War, this spot was a social gathering place. During the Civil War (when this photo was taken) it served as a military prison where Pres. Abraham Lincoln is said to have visited Confederate prisoners-of-war. Lincoln suspended the writ of habeas corpus during the war, whereby anyone suspected of even the mildest sympathies toward the Confederacy could be arrested and detained at will by the military without the benefit of legal representation or judicial recourse. After the Civil War, the building served as a parking garage, more than one restaurant, a karate school, and the current clothing store.

Abraham Lincoln, 1809–1865, 16th President of the United States. There are several memorials to this assassinated president in Washington, D.C. Besides the Lincoln Memorial on the West Mall, visit a smaller statue at Judiciary Square on D Street between Fourth and Fifth Streets, NW, and Abe Lincoln the Rail Splitter in the Department of the Interior Building on C Street between Eighteenth and Nineteenth Streets, NW.

Site B21: Stohlman's Confectionary at 1254 Wisconsin Avenue. If you have the chance to visit the American History Museum in Washington, D.C., stop by the Hall of Everyday Life. There you will find on permanent display (below) a part of the ice cream parlor belonging to Stohlman's Confectionary that was located here from 1865 to 1957. First, the building housed Arnold's Bakery beginning in 1820, then Frederick Stohlman established an ice cream parlor that quickly became an extremely popular place in Georgetown, providing a place for social gatherings. The building served as an ice cream parlor as late as the early 1990s.

Stohlman's Confectionary Counters at the American History Museum, Washington, D.C., June 1999. Ice cream was created in Europe about 1735, and legend has it that President Thomas Jefferson was the first to introduce this new frozen dessert to guests at the White House during his administration. The ice cream cone came into being about 1900 and was originally made from waffles formed by hand.

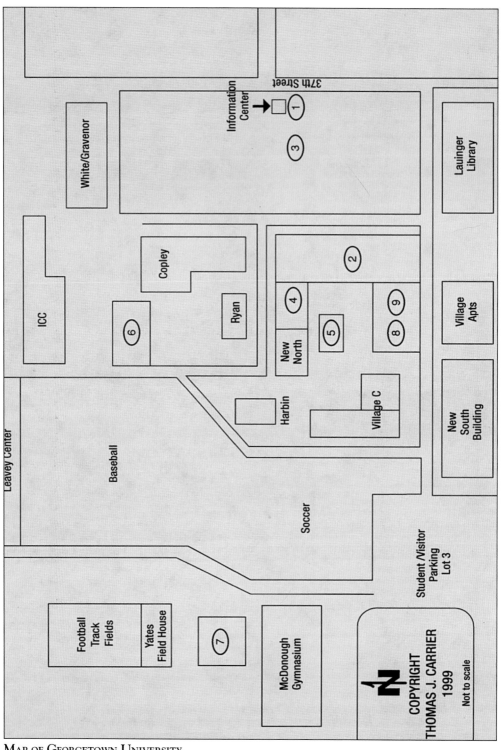

Map of Georgetown University.

Tour C

GEORGETOWN

UNIVERSITY

When Bishop John Carroll wanted to establish a school for students of "every Religious Profession," he almost considered the site where the U.S. Capitol now stands. Luckily, he thought that the area was entirely "too far into the country." Indeed, he was right. With the port of George near the spot on which the school was founded, some semblance of civilization was close at hand.

Still, the Potomac River bluff Carroll chose continues to have the best view of any site in Washington. Healy Hall represents Georgetown University well and is a distinguished landmark known up and down the Potomac River. On any given summer day, sculls race along the Potomac River and continue a university tradition that stretches back over 200 years.

This is by no means a complete tour of the Georgetown University campus. This format only allows for the representation of a certain number of historical sites, such as Healy Hall, the Old North building, and Dahlgren Chapel. We're also fortunate that there are some surviving images of such sites as the Old South building (the original building) and the Infirmary Gardens, both of which are now long gone. They evoke an earlier period of Georgetown history that should not be forgotten.

Many distinguished Americans have been associated with this historic campus and have left their mark through the last 200 years. Pres. George Washington addressed students from Old North, and Pres. William Jefferson Clinton received his law degree here. Visit other sites throughout the university beyond the historical ones, if you can. Just be aware that this is a working campus.

SITE C1: GEORGETOWN UNIVERSITY BUILDINGS, 1850. In the 1800s, this area was popularly known as "Holy Hill" because of the proximity of the Catholic institutions surrounding Georgetown University, a Jesuit institution. As a college, Georgetown was created from land selected by the Reverend John Carroll in 1788 and bought in 1789 from John Threlkeld and William Deakins. Although William Gaston, only 13 years old, was the first student to enroll in 1791, the year 1789 is considered to be Georgetown University's founding year. Many of the students today are not Catholic.

THE REVEREND JOHN CARROLL, FOUNDER OF GEORGETOWN UNIVERSITY, 1789. By 1830, the college informed its students that they needed to bring ". . . a mattress, a pillow, two pillow cases, two pairs of sheets, four blankets . . . one suit of clothes for a uniform . . . two suits for daily wear . . . six shirts, six pairs of stockings, six pocket handkerchiefs, three pairs of shoes, a hat and a cloak or great coat, also a silver spoon. These articles if not brought by the student will be furnished by the college and included in the first bill."

WILLIAM GASTON, THE FIRST STUDENT OF GEORGETOWN UNIVERSITY, 1791. This photo shows Gaston after a distinguished career as a member of Congress from North Carolina and a justice of the Supreme Court of that state. When he enrolled in Georgetown College, he lived and took classes in the Old South building, the only one on campus in 1789.

AN AERIAL VIEW OF GEORGETOWN UNIVERSITY CAMPUS, C. 1920. This image was used to help raise funds for additional campus buildings. Clockwise from the bottom left are Healy Hall, Copley Hall, and White/Gravenor Hall. The cornerstone for the last building, facing Thirty-seventh Street, was never laid due to the onset of the Depression in 1929.

SITE C2: HEALY HALL. The building was named for the Rt. Rev. Patrick F. Healy, S.J., considered to be the second founder of Georgetown University after Bishop John Carroll. It is rather European, and the American Institute of Architects describes it as "this baronial fantasy." Healy Hall is constructed of Potomac gneiss walls at 4.5 stories tall. Built in 1877, the 200-foot-tall clock tower presides over all of Georgetown University and can be seen as a landmark up and down the Potomac River.

SITE C3: BISHOP JOHN CARROLL STATUE. The founder of Georgetown College and the first archbishop of Baltimore, the Most Reverend John Carroll, D.D., LL.D., was born in Prince George's County, Maryland, in 1735. His cousin, Charles Carroll of Carrollton, was a signer of the Declaration of Independence; his brother Daniel signed the Constitution. In 1785, John Carroll proposed the plan for the college, and building began in 1788. The first student, William Gaston, would not formally enroll until 1791. Bishop Carroll would live to see his college become a university in May 1815, but he died in December of that year. The 6-foot-high bronze statue designed by Jerome Connor was dedicated here in 1912.

Site C4: Old North Building. The Old North Building, just behind the Healy Building, was built between 1791 and 1808 and is the only original building dating to the days when Georgetown was a college. Two acres of land were bought from John Threlkeld (Site D11), and, to pay for the building, property was sold and some beef was exchanged to make up the difference. From this front porch, George Washington addressed the students in 1797; the Marquis de Lafayette did the same in 1824. This sketch was made in 1932 for the yearbook and shows a covered porch that did not exist during Washington's time.

Site C5: Dahlgren Chapel. The chapel is named for Joseph Drexel Dahlgren, son of school benefactors John (an 1889 graduate) and Elizabeth Dahlgren. The cornerstone was laid on May 19, 1892, by James Cardinal Gibbons and completed in 1894. The chapel, officially known as the Chapel of the Sacred Heart of Jesus, seats 500 and is 109 feet long and 60 feet wide at the transepts.

SITE C6: CEMETERY. Since the early 19th century, this has been the final resting place for members of the Jesuit community, who have served Georgetown University. Several gravesites indicate burials that took place as early as the late 1820s, but a cemetery has existed here since 1808. The Reverend Patrick Healy (Site C2) is buried here. The photo was taken about 1920.

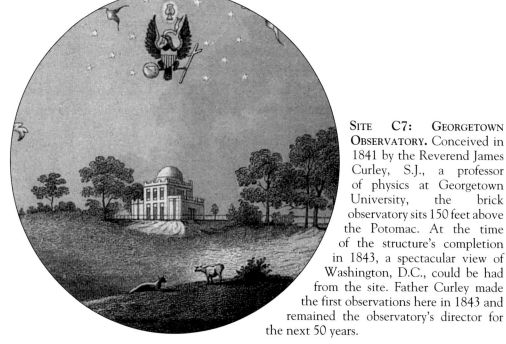

SITE C7: GEORGETOWN OBSERVATORY. Conceived in 1841 by the Reverend James Curley, S.J., a professor of physics at Georgetown University, the brick observatory sits 150 feet above the Potomac. At the time of the structure's completion in 1843, a spectacular view of Washington, D.C., could be had from the site. Father Curley made the first observations here in 1843 and remained the observatory's director for the next 50 years.

SITE C8: INFIRMARY GARDEN. Fr. Thomas Mulledy, president of Georgetown College in 1830, built an infirmary especially for Georgetown students. The west section was completed in 1830, but the east section was not finished until 1848. A 6-foot-high, zinc statue, representing St. Joseph and the Child Jesus, was placed in the Infirmary Gardens by university students to celebrate no student losses during the smallpox epidemic of 1873. The completion of Ryan Hall in 1904 required the removal of the garden, but the Infirmary remains. The current statue of St. Joseph replaced the original when it broke in the 1980s.

SITE C9: SOUTH BUILDING. The first original building of Georgetown College was located here. Begun in 1788, it served as an academy of offices and classrooms. Bishop Carroll wrote to a friend on March 1, 1788, saying "We shall begin the building of our Academy this summer. In the beginning we shall confine our plan to a house of 63 or 64 by 50 feet [and] be 3 stories high . . ." The building was razed in 1904 to build the Ida M. Ryan Hall and the Ryan gymnasium. The photo of the Infirmary Garden (above), taken about 1900, actually shows the back of the original South Building.

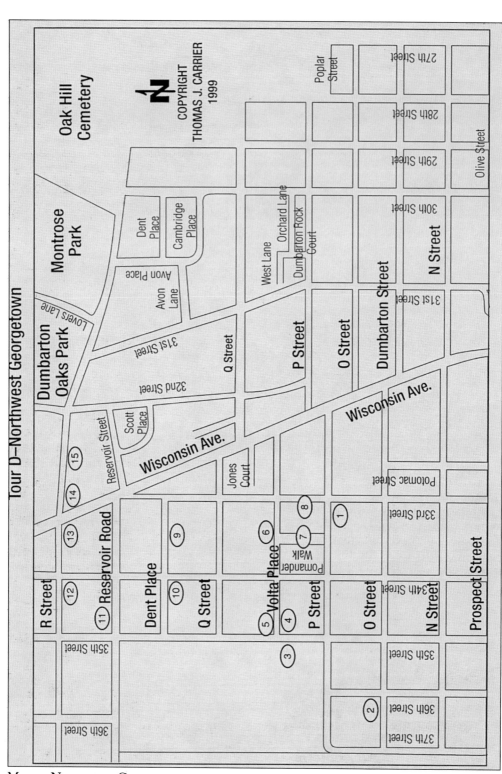

MAP OF NORTHWEST GEORGETOWN.

Tour D

NORTHWEST GEORGETOWN

You are now entering a typical Georgetown neighborhood. Many of these homes and businesses date back to the mid-19th century. However, the historic character of this neighborhood is quite unlike any other, as you will see.

Georgetown University still dominates this area, and the Visitation Convent has its headquarters nearby on Thirty-fifth Street, though the trees and woods hide it well. This area was known as Hawkins' and Beatty's Addition before 1751, and, like Threlkeld's Addition on the site of Georgetown University, this entire area remained undeveloped until the early 18th century.

Alexander Graham Bell lived here and experimented with the "graphaphone" in a garage owned by his equally famous father. Nearby, a historic old tavern welcomed visitors to Georgetown, but not just any visitors—the kind able to pay for a room of their own, a quite unusual occurrence in the 18th century. You will meet the family who owned the infamous Hope Diamond, now on display at the American History Museum on the Mall. Edward Kennedy Ellington, "Duke" to his friends, is represented here, too. We'll also visit Pomander Walk, an alleyway that is completely restored today, but as early as the 1950s represented the economic divide between the "haves" and the "have nots" of Washington.

We'll begin our tour on a site that pre-dates the founding of Georgetown by at least a generation. Later, as you continue your walk, you'll be able to visit the center of neighborhood life since its beginning—the corner store. You can refresh yourself there.

Site D1: Yellow House at 1430 Thirty-third Street. Here is a unique old brick house that dates to about 1810. A wood-frame house had occupied this site beginning in 1733, according to the Work Projects Administration (WPA) Guide of Washington, D.C. If true, this brick house probably replaced it. This house may have been associated with the Yellow Tavern located down the street, although its complete history is rather obscure. More importantly, the house sits on a parcel of land known as "Knaves Disappointment." Along with George Beall, George Gordon was the original landowner of this property and other parcels that would become Georgetown in 1752. Georgetown was probably not named for them; it was more likely named for King George III of England.

Site D2: Thirty-sixth and O Streets. This is an earlier image of this busy intersection taken about the 1950s. Just to the left of this photo at the corner with the white brick front was a general store that is now a private home. Healy Hall is still prominent in the background.

SITE D3: GEORGETOWN CONVENT OF THE VISITATION OF THE HOLY MARY AT 1500 THIRTY-FIFTH STREET. Situated on landowner Henry Threlkeld's estate known as Berlieth, this house existed from about 1716 to about 1782. Established here in 1789 on 40 acres by the Rt. Rev. Leonard Neale, the first president of Georgetown University, the convent was recognized in 1816 by Pope Pius VII as the Order of the Visitation, a teaching order. The order itself was founded in 1610 by Francis de Sales at Annecy, France, and dedicated to St. Martha, the patron saint of the poor.

THRELKELD STABLES, C. 1900

SITE D4: MELVILLE BELL HOUSE AT 1527 THIRTY-FIFTH STREET. Facing the Visitation Convent was the antebellum residence of Alexander Melville Bell, whose son Alexander Graham Bell perfected the graphaphone in an experimental laboratory, now a garage, after he moved here in 1879. Bell Sr. was a teacher of elocution in Scotland and later in London and Ontario, Canada. He developed the "physiological alphabet" in which the articulating position of the vocal cords for each sound was visually presented. Bell Sr.'s son was his assistant and, later, a teacher of his methods. Bell Sr. died in 1905 at the age of 86.

ALEXANDER GRAHAM BELL. Bell went on to open a school for the deaf in Boston in 1872; he patented the telegraph in 1875 and the telephone a year later. He helped form the Bell Telephone Co. in 1877 prior to his moving here in 1879. Alexander Graham Bell continued to advance on additional patents and other experiments. He founded the journal *Science* in 1883 and was the president of the National Geographic Society from 1896 to 1904. Bell died in 1922 at the age of 75.

SITE D5: VOLTA BUREAU AT 1537 THIRTY-FIFTH STREET. After moving to the United States in 1879, Alexander Graham Bell established the Volta Bureau the following year with the Volta Prize of $10,000 he was awarded for his invention of the telephone and other patents. The prize was named for the Italian physicist and inventor of the electric battery, Count Alessandro Volta, by Napoleon I. Here, the American Association to Promote the Teaching of Speech to the Deaf was established in 1890. Helen Keller broke ground for this current building on May 8, 1893.

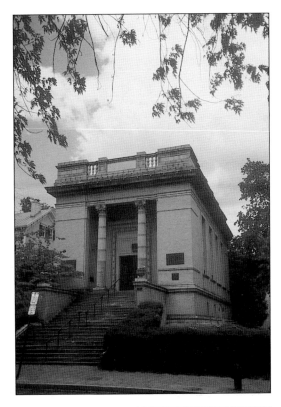

SITE D6: PRESBYTERIAN BURIAL GROUND ON THE SQUARE BOUNDED BY O AND P STREETS AND WISCONSIN AND THIRTY-FIFTH STREETS. One of the earliest cemeteries in Washington, D.C., was dedicated in 1802 (this early sketch is a representation only). Romulus Riggs, Col. Urriah Forrest, Benjamin Mackall, William Marbury, and Thomas Beall, all early founders of Georgetown, were interred here. The cemetery had nearly 70 tombs and nearly 2,700 individual gravesites surrounded by a 9-foot-high brick wall. As early as 1871, the cemetery was overgrown and neglected. In 1907, local residents acted by closing the cemetery, removing the burial plots mostly to Oak Hill Cemetery, and creating the Volta Playground.

SITE D7: POMANDER WALK, AN ALLEY ON VOLTA PLACE BETWEEN THIRTY-THIRD AND THIRTY-FOURTH STREETS. Turn left from Volta Place into an alley that would not be recognizable only 50 years ago. Known as Bell Court, the area was home to 40 African-American families until their eviction by the District of Columbia in 1950. They worked mostly as domestics, construction workers, and in other low-income jobs. These additional photographs of alleys in Washington, D.C., were probably taken in the 1940s and show the conditions of alley life at that time.

ALLEY DWELLINGS. As early as 1870, the District of Columbia Board of Health worked to eliminate alley dwellings. These areas were generally without water, heat, electricity, and sewage and had a tendency to become overcrowded. In 1914, alley dwellings were to be outlawed after 1918, but enforcement was rare. In 1934, Congress created the Alley Dwelling Elimination Act that bought alleys for "conversion to other uses" while building low-cost housing elsewhere for those displaced. By the 1950s, alley housing was virtually eliminated.

CONVERTED SINGLE-FAMILY HOMES AND APARTMENTS. As you walk throughout Georgetown you will see stables, alleyways, and carriage houses all lovingly converted into very appealing, single-family homes and apartments. Something earlier residents would not have recognized.

SITE D8: YELLOW TAVERN AT 1524 THIRTY-THIRD STREET. An 18th-century English actor named John Bernard described traveling at that time in the following way: "A mile's ride was about the most powerful experiment on one's anatomy a man could desire." Unpaved streets proved impassable after a rainstorm, and the Yellow Tavern, known later as the White Horse Inn, was a most gracious respite from the difficulties of travel. Built in the early 1800s, it was originally two buildings that were joined much later. Normally, guests in taverns shared beds with strangers, the "privy" was outside, meals were unreliable, and bathing was done only during the holidays. Here, the living was of a higher quality in order to attract the likes of Thomas Jefferson.

SITE D9: MAMOUT RESIDENCE AT 3330–3332 DENT PLACE. Yarrow Mamout was an emancipated slave set free by Upton Beall in 1807 when Mamout was 45. Beall promised that "[he] hath my security that he shall not become a [bother] of the County of Washington." Mamout had the fortune to sit for the celebrated portrait painter Charles Wilson Peale in 1819 for a painting that is now part of the Peabody Collection of the Georgetown Public Library. Mamout is reported to have lived over 100 years.

SITE D10: OLD GENERAL STORE ON THE SOUTHWEST CORNER OF DENT PLACE AND THIRTY-FOURTH STREET. Before there were large supermarkets, the corner store satisfied a neighborhood's household and grocery needs. During the 18th and early 19th centuries, the open-air markets, such as the old Center Market in Washington, D.C. (now the National Archives building), was where locals got fresh vegetables and meat. This store has been here since the 1930s, but the current owner now lives out of state. Come in for something refreshing.

CENTER MARKET, C. 1920S.

SITE D11: DUKE ELLINGTON SCHOOL OF THE ARTS AT THIRTY-FIFTH AND R STREETS. This is the only four-year, public school in Washington, D.C., dedicated to dance, music, drama, and the visual arts. Nearly 80 percent of graduates continue their education at the renowned Juilliard, the Pratt Institute of Art, or the Rhode Island School of Design. The school was formerly Western High School. Edward Kennedy Ellington was born in 1899 in Washington, D.C., and became a famous bandleader and composer of such hits as "Don't Get Around Much Anymore," "Sophisticated Lady," and "Mood Indigo." He also wrote movie scores for such films as *Black, Brown, and Beige* in 1943 and *Harlem* in 1950. Ellington died in 1974 at the age of 75.

THE CEDARS. The Cedars stood on this site as a part of the John Threlkeld estate dating to 1716. Threlkeld's daughter Jane married John Cox, the mayor of Georgetown when they married in 1822. The couple built The Cedars as their home, and it was later incorporated into the Convent of the Visitation. This photo was shot in the sun c. 1900.

SITE D12: CENTURY HOUSE AT 3406 R STREET. The land on which this house was built in 1820 was given as a dowry when Leonard Mackall married Catherine Beall, the daughter of Brooke Beall, a member of one of Georgetown's founding families and a successful grain and tobacco shipping merchant. Leonard's brother Benjamin married Beall's other daughter, Christiana, and the couple were given the Rock of Dumbarton, also known as Mackall Square (Site F22). Both the Mackalls and the Bealls were some of the earliest and most prominent families in Georgetown history. This house was renamed Century House by the wife of Frank West, who owned the property early in this century.

Leonard Mackall   Mrs. Leonard Mackall

SITE D13: MCLEAN ESTATE AT 3300 WISCONSIN AVENUE. Evalyn Walsh McLean, a Washington hostess "extraordinaire," entertained lavishly, as would befit the owner of the infamous Hope Diamond, a 44-carat, blue diamond that some believe to be cursed. After the "country estate" was sold (see below), Mrs. McLean moved here, renamed the home Friendship, and remained until her death in 1947. Together, the McLeans had wiped out both family fortunes totaling about $100 million—mostly on entertainment and travel.

EDWARD AND EVALYN WALSH MCLEAN. John McLean, for whom the town of McLean, Virginia, is named, left his son Edward a fortune when he died in 1916. Edward inherited a "country estate" known as Friendship on Wisconsin Avenue, shown here before being razed for McLean Gardens in 1942. Edward McLean married Evalyn Walsh, the daughter of Sen. Thomas Walsh of Colorado and a successful silver miner. The couple entertained and traveled extravagantly until Edward was affected by the Teapot Dome scandal during the Harding administration of the early 1920s. McLean died in 1941, his reputation destroyed and his fortune lost.

SITE D14: WISCONSIN AVENUE RESERVOIR ON THE SOUTHEAST CORNER OF WISCONSIN AVENUE AND R STREET. Water was stored here for use by residents of Georgetown and the rest of Washington, D.C. This high-service reservoir, built in 1859 by Gen. Montgomery C. Meigs, was a high-domed brick building, 120 feet in diameter and 50 feet high. By 1897, other high-service reservoirs had come into operation, making this one obsolete. It was finally razed in 1932 to build the Georgetown branch of the D.C. Public Library. The surrounding stone walls and the name of Reservoir Road are the only reminders of this great engineering feat.

SITE D15: HALLECK HOUSE AT 3238 R STREET. This was the home of Gen. Henry W. Halleck, the chief-of-staff of the army during the Civil War. Halleck was an effective administrator, but somewhat less effective as a tactician or strategist. He died as the commander of the Division of the South in 1872 at the age of 52. Gen. Ulysses Grant lived in this home after the Civil War and until his election to the presidency in 1872. During the presidency of Franklin Roosevelt, this house, known as the "big red house on R Street," was a gathering place for Roosevelt's "brain trust" of personal advisors. The house is a private residence today.

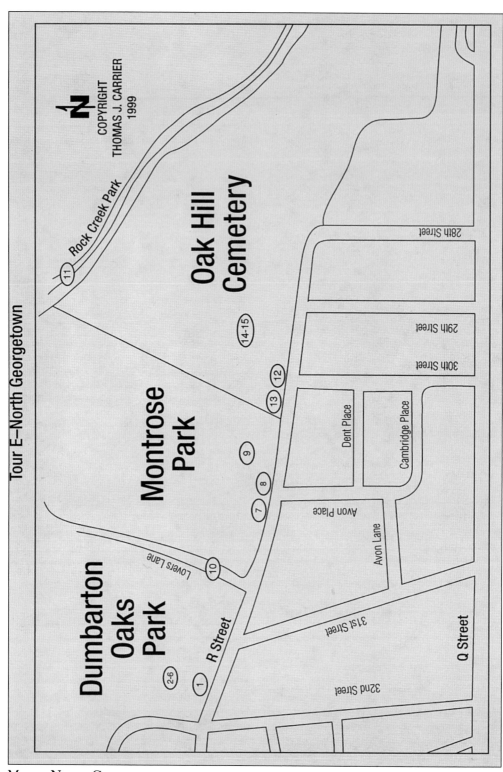

MAP OF NORTH GEORGETOWN.

Tour E

North Georgetown

There are only three very distinctive sites to visit on this tour: Dumbarton Oaks, Melrose Park, and Oak Hill Cemetery. If you take the time to visit each of them, you will have covered a lot of ground.

Dumbarton Oaks is one of the largest original grants still left in Georgetown. Very much reduced from its original size, the area is still a historic treasure. For, you see, this is the famed Rock of Dumbarton, the site Col. Ninian Beall chose as his homestead in his adopted country. When you visit here you will also find a pre-Columbian art museum, sweeping gardens, and wonderful pathways that lead, well, everywhere.

When you leave Dumbarton Oaks, you can rest in Montrose Park just next door. It is a wide-open space dedicated to picnicking, outdoor games, and barbecues. Its early history as a "rope walk" will add an entirely new dimension to your visit. Or, if you need more adventure, take Lovers Lane and walk along a trail that leads you along the Rock Creek and all the way to the National Zoo if you like.

Now, fully rested, you will be able to walk next door and visit Oak Hill Cemetery. Here, Georgetown's early citizens and neighbors are resting comfortably. A map at the gatehouse will provide a more detailed walking tour, but you will no doubt see the names of many individuals you have met or will meet throughout this tour.

SITE E1: DUMBARTON OAKS AT 1703 THIRTY-SECOND STREET. Originally, the Rock of Dumbarton, named so by its first owner Col. Ninian Beall, covered 495 acres of mostly woodland about 1800. Today, only 16 acres remain, which are filled with gardens and a very expansive Georgian Revival–style mansion. There have been many changes throughout the Rock of Dumbarton's history, but only a total of eight owners, including its present owner, Harvard University.

MONTEREY. Georgetown merchant Edward Linthicum owned Monterey, as he called it, from 1846 until 1891. During this time, the house took on the Second Empire style, but it was removed by Robert Woods Bliss in 1921. The house was used as a setting for the famous Dumbarton Oaks Conference in August 1944 that helped to usher in the United Nations. Today, Monterey serves Harvard University as the Dumbarton Oaks Research Library and Collection of Byzantine and pre-Columbian artifacts. *Open from April to October, 2 p.m. to 6 p.m.; from November to March, 2 p.m. to 5 p.m. Admission fee. Call (202) 339-6401 for more information.*

MRS. NINIAN BEALL

ROCK OF DUMBARTON. Col. and Mrs. Ninian Beall, the first owners of the Rock of Dumbarton, named the 795-acre Maryland tract after a site in Col. Beall's native Glasgow, Scotland. Col. Beall owned over 30,000 acres, and this area was completely undeveloped during his lifetime. George Beall, the couple's son, owned the eastern portion of the original Town of George (now Georgetown) in 1751.

SITE E2: PEBBLE GARDEN. This delightful and intricate garden replaced a tennis court in the early 1960s. The stone used here is from Mexico. The sculptures of putti and seahorses are 3 feet high and were probably made about 1800. They were brought originally from Paris in 1933 for the Meridian House but were instead installed here in 1959. Like all of the gardens in Dumbarton Oaks, the Pebble Garden was designed by noted landscape architect Beatrix Ferrand.

SITE E3: WINTER AND SITE E4: SPHINX. *Winter* (at left) is a late-18th-century lead on teakwood sculpture located in the Orangery. *Sphinx* (below) is an early-19th-century terra cotta sculpture also located in the Orangery. Most of the sculptures in the gardens were designed by Beatrix Farrand and sculpted by Frederick Coles.

SITE E5: DUMBARTON OAKS GARDENS. These formal gardens cover 10 acres and were created after the Bliss family moved here in 1921. Prior to the creation of the gardens, this entire area was mostly undeveloped pastureland with a wonderful, unobstructed view of downtown Washington, D.C. The stone in all of the gardens comes from quarries in Maryland, Virginia, Tennessee, Pennsylvania, and Italy. Visit the museum shop for more complete information about these gardens and the property.

SITE E6: DUMBARTON OAKS RESEARCH LIBRARY AT THE THIRTY-SECOND STREET ENTRANCE. The photograph is dated 1943, about a year after the construction of this library, which was designed by Thomas Waterman, a well-known architect of embassies and other buildings in and around Washington, D.C. The gate to the right of the building no longer exists but, at the time, was a service gate to the main house. The building is now the public entrance to the Byzantine Collection and Garden Library.

SITE E7: MONTROSE PARK ON R STREET AT AVON PLACE. Richard Parrott, a rope manufacturer, built a Federal-style house here in 1810. By 1837, William Boyce, the new owner, had named his estate Montrose to honor the Scottish earls of Montrose. Boyce died in an accident in 1858, at which time his wife moved to England. The house remained virtually abandoned until 1911 when it was razed to build Montrose Park, now managed by the National Park Service.

SITE E8: RITTENHOUSE GARDEN AT THE ENTRANCE TO MONTROSE PARK. Sarah Louisa Rittenhouse, "Miss Loulie," worked tirelessly to create a public park here. She grew up at Dumbarton House (Site F18) and remembers the picnics and the special events that occurred here. By 1910, the government purchased the lot to create Montrose Park. The house, though, could not be saved. Today, the Rittenhouse Garden, named for "Miss Loulie," stands where Montrose once stood. Rittenhouse is buried in Oak Hill Cemetery just next door. The Georgetown Garden Club placed the bronze armillary sphere here in her memory in 1956.

SITE E9: PARROTT'S ROPEWALK. Originally known as Parrott's Woods, this area was named for Richard Parrott, the owner of a ropewalk. Here, hemp was twisted by hand to form the thick cords of rope used by ship owners to secure their commercial vessels at the docks nearby. According to Christian Hines, there were two ropewalks in Washington, and, by the War of 1812, there were about six rope walks in Washington, D.C., including the one originally located here. On August 24, 1814, the British burned the ropewalk of Ringgold and Heath on the Mall near Seventh Street; it had been in business for only ten days. For more detailed information on Parrott's Ropewalk and how ropes were made and used for shipping, visit the National Park Service display here in Montrose Park.

SITE E10: LOVERS LANE, AN ALLEY SEPARATING MONTROSE PARK AND DUMBARTON OAKS. Originally part of the Dumbarton Oaks estate, this unimproved road quietly runs behind Dumbarton Oaks and continues until it meets up with Rock Creek Park. Along the way are unspoiled wilderness, streams, and walking trails. This part of the original Dumbarton Oaks estate, about 27 acres, was donated to the National Park Service in 1940. The National Park Service owns and maintains the trails.

SITE E11: ROCK CREEK PARK. With the enormous growth of Washington, D.C., in the last 50 years, it is hard to imagine the time, which stretched well after the Civil War, when most of the city was wilderness. As you continue down Lovers Lane, pick up a brochure near the bottom and visit the miles of walking trails that lead directly into the last unspoiled place in the District of Columbia. Maintained by the National Park Service, Rock Creek wends its way more than 4 miles from the zoo throughout the city, covering more than 1,800 acres. It is said that Theodore Roosevelt visited Rock Creek often during his presidency. On September 27, 1890, Congress authorized the purchase of the entire Rock Creek valley as a "pleasuring ground for the benefit and enjoyment of the people of the United States." Visit the area about which Lord James Bryce, British Ambassador to the United States from 1907 to 1913, once said "there is nothing comparable in any capital city of Europe."

ROCK CREEK NEAR M STREET, C. EARLY 1900S.

ROCK CREEK WITH HORSE RIDING STABLES UNDER ONE OF THE MANY BRIDGES SPANNING ROCK CREEK.

SITE E12: OAK HILL CEMETERY AT 3001 R STREET. Prior to the establishment of Oak Hill Cemetery in 1849, the major cemetery in Georgetown was the Presbyterian Burial Ground between O and P Streets (Site D6). By 1848, though, the cemetery was in such a state of neglect that philanthropist William W. Corcoran bought 15 acres from George Corbin Washington, a great nephew of George Washington, and created Oak Hill Cemetery. Here, many original landowners, Revolutionary War patriots, and distinguished Americans of our early history have been laid to rest. The history of America lies here. *Open Monday-Friday, 10 a.m. to 4 p.m. Closed on weekends and national holidays. Pick up a map at the office and please observe the rules posted at the gate, including no photography.*

SITE E13: GATEHOUSE. George de la Roche designed this imposing brick and sandstone, Italianate gatehouse for Oak Hill Cemetery in 1850. The original bell was replaced in 1993 and now rests just inside the gate to the right.

Site E14: Gothic Chapel. Designed by famed architect James Renwick Jr. in 1850, this simple, Gothic-style, stone chapel has red sandstone trim. Because we are used to seeing grander designs from Renwick, such as the Smithsonian Castle on the Mall, the Renwick Gallery of American Art near Lafayette Square, and St. Patrick's Cathedral in New York City, we are surprised that a simple chapel would even be worth his time. But it is a perfect structure in a perfect setting and is certainly worth the visit.

Site E15: Van Ness Mausoleum. Here, George Hadfield designed a miniature Temple of Vesta at Rome to memorialize one of the first families of Washington, D.C., the Van Ness family. Created in 1833, the mausoleum, like so many others, was moved from the family's private burying ground from the site of the Department of Justice building near Tenth and M Streets. Marcia Van Ness was the daughter of David Burnes, on whose land the White House now sits. Marcia married New York Congressman John Peter Van Ness, and they, together with their daughter Anne Middleton, are buried here.

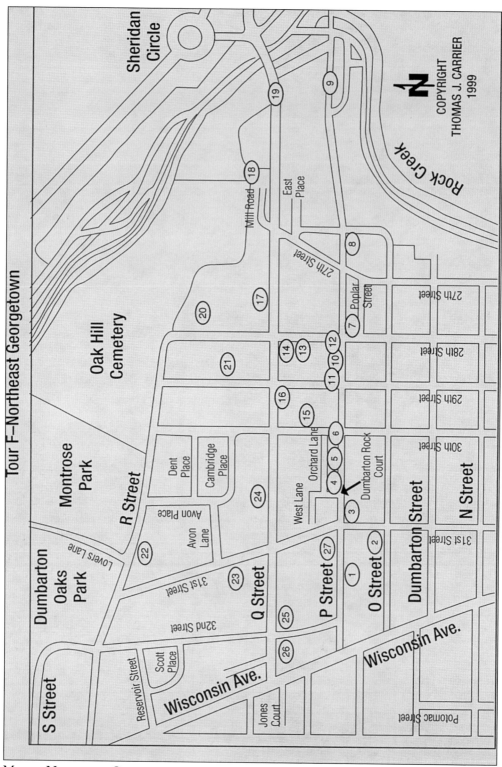

MAP OF NORTHEAST GEORGETOWN.

Tour F

NORTHEAST
GEORGETOWN

Back in the late 18th century, all of this area north of N Street was underdeveloped. As you walk through this area, you will find large estates that date back to this era still standing. The Mackalls and the Dodges were both well-known families and part of Georgetown society in the 19th century. Though the interiors of Evermay, the Dodge home, and the Mackall House cannot be visited, the homes provide visual proof of the historic links these families have with the past. On the other hand, Tudor Place, the home of Martha Parke Custis, a step-granddaughter to George Washington, is open to the public. Here, you will get a rare chance to visit a grand residence of the very early 19th century.

Nearby is the old Mt. Zion cemetery. Unused now, it rivaled, just briefly, the Oak Hill Cemetery on the other side of the fence. Its story will take you back to a segregated society that extended even to the grave.

If you've ever visited a government auction, you must have gotten some great bargains. Imagine bringing home several dozen muskets that became government surplus just after the Mexican War of 1848. What would you do with them? Well, continue your tour and find out what one homeowner did with his.

SITE F1: SHOEMAKER HOUSE AT 3116 P STREET. The flour mill business was pretty good for George Shoemaker, a Quaker from Lancaster County, Pennsylvania. As an inspector, Shoemaker was responsible for certifying the several flour mills operating in and around the C&O Canal. He built this house about 1831. In *Georgetown Life*, a house at 3121 O Street is also designated as a Shoemaker house, but it was built in 1874, indicating that Shoemaker may have moved here later in life. No other information is available.

SITE F2: BERRY HOUSE, 1402 31ST STREET. This brings us to another example of how misleading historical information can be perpetuated, sometimes for generations. Philip T. Berry built this house about 1865. The story goes that a congressman or senator from Maine covered the brick walls with a wooden frame to disguise the fact that he lived in a more expensive brick house. During renovations in the 1950s, though, no brick was found. When someone finally checked the land records, it was discovered that there was never a tenant or owner of this building who was a member of Congress. Who began this story we'll never know.

SITE F3: BROWN HOUSE AT 3044 P STREET. Emma V. Brown was instrumental in the education of the African-American children of Washington, D.C., during and after the Civil War. In 1864, Brown became one of only two teachers in the only public school created for African Americans; it was located in the Ebenezer Methodist Church on Capitol Hill. By 1871, Brown was the principal of Sumner School in Washington, D.C.

SITE F4: ROWHOUSES AT 3022–3034 P STREET. This series of Federal-style townhomes were built in 1818. These townhouses were rather wide, by today's standards, and their value was originally assessed at $4,000. Today, their worth is nearly $750,000. Who knew?

SITE F5: LINTHICUM HOUSE AT 3019 P STREET. This was, in effect, a starter house for the successful Georgetown merchant Edward Linthicum of Linthicum's Hardware Store at Wisconsin and M Street (Site G1). He built this house in 1829, but, after more success, moved to Dumbarton Oaks in 1846, then called the Oaks, for which he payed $11,000. Linthicum became a member of the town council and a trustee of the Methodist church. He established the Linthicum Institute, a school "for the free education of white boys in Georgetown" in the old Curtis school next to St. John's Church.

SITE F6: MORGAN BROS. PHARMACY AT 3001 P STREET. According to the current owner of the building, two brothers named Morgan started this pharmacy about 150 years ago. The early telephone directories of Washington, D.C., place the Morgan Pharmacy no earlier than 1913 at this address. Prior to 1913, this address appears to have been owned by Sarah A.C. Welsh. She was affiliated with the Louise Home, dedicated to the "education and refinement of young women." The home was founded in 1870 by William W. Corcoran in memory of his daughter Louise, and its headquarters were at Massachusetts Avenue and Fifteenth Street.

SITE F7: GRIFFIN MARKET AT TWENTY-EIGHTH AND P STREETS. This is just an example of one of the fixtures of neighborhood life in Georgetown since its early days. While the current owners aren't too sure how long the store has been in operation, the building itself, with its corrugated roof, obviously has been here since the early 1900s. You will see additional corner stores as you walk through Georgetown, reminding you of penny candies, barrels of flour, and neighborhood gossip.

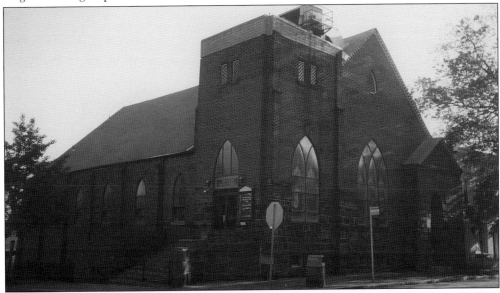

SITE F8: JERUSALEM BAPTIST CHURCH AT 2600 P STREET. This is a sister church to the First Baptist Church located at Twenty-seventh Street and Dumbarton Avenue (Site G12). The number of Baptists in the area had increased significantly enough by 1870 that Rev. Sandy Alexander of the First Baptist Church founded this church in that year and named it the Seventh Baptist Church. This "new" brick church was built in 1903, and its name was changed to the Jerusalem Baptist Church.

SITE F9: P STREET BRIDGE AT THE EAST END OF P STREET. There has been a bridge here since before the new Federal City was built. In fact, Christian Hines mentions that until the M Street Bridge was built, this was the only way to get from Georgetown to the new Federal City. At one time, a paper mill stood nearby, and this was known as the Paper Mill Bridge. On P Street between Twenty-second and Twenty-third Streets stood the Washington Riding Academy. From 1888 until it was razed in 1936 for a gas station, a huge, 13,000-square-foot, stucco brick building brought riding lessons to the elite and to the common people of Washington, D.C.

SITE F10: DAW ROW AT 2803–2805, 2811 P STREET AND 1516–1518 TWENTY-EIGHTH STREET. Reuben Daw built all of these residences, and the P Street homes date to the 1840s. Daw lived at 1516 Twenty-eighth Street, which he had built for himself in 1853. The captain of the U.S. battleship *Maine*, Admiral Sigsbee, lived at 2811 P Street until the tragic accident in Havana harbor in 1898 that began U.S. involvement in the Spanish-American War. Former Secretary of State Dean Acheson lived at 2805 P Street during the administration of Pres. Harry S. Truman.

100

SITE F11: ALEXANDER HAMILTON DODGE HOUSE AT 2819 P STREET. This was the home of Alexander Hamilton Dodge, the son of Francis Dodge. Though the house was built about 1830, Dodge didn't move in with his family until 1855. The wedding of his daughter in 1873 proved that he lived in this house for at least a generation. The Dodge warehouse still exists in Georgetown owing to the great care of the family business.

SITE F12: GUNBARREL FENCE AT 1516–1518 TWENTY-EIGHTH STREET. We're back once again at this address because you might notice something unusual about the fence surrounding these Daw homes. That's right. Reuben Daw found a bargain at auction on quite a few military surplus gun barrels. When the Mexican War ended in 1848, the government had an abundance of these items and he used them to create a fence around his property—with the stock down. I think the spikes in the muzzles are a nice touch.

SITE F13: MILLER HOUSE AT 1524 TWENTY-EIGHTH STREET. Built about 1840, this clapboard New England–style home belonged to Benjamin F. Miller, a construction engineer who designed the Aqueduct Bridge across the Potomac River to Arlington, Virginia. This style was quite unusual compared to the usually Federal or Georgian architectural styles of Miller's neighbors. The six-panel front door with transom, for example, is definitely a New England characteristic.

SITE F14: ROBERT DODGE HOUSE AT TWENTY-EIGHTH AND Q STREETS. Francis Dodge was considered the richest man in Georgetown when he died in 1851. He had 11 children, 6 of them boys. Alexander Hamilton Dodge (Site F11) was son number two; Robert Dodge was son number three. Robert Dodge lived here in this Italianate-style house when it was built in 1850. The house was severely remodeled in 1929 and 1936 to include Gothic Revival and neo-Georgian influences. The original landscaping was designed by Andrew Jackson Downing, the famed designer of the grounds of the Mall and the U.S. Capitol.

Site F15: Frances Dodge Jr. House at 1517 Thirtieth Street. This is virtually an identical twin to the Robert Dodge House at Twenty-eighth and Q Streets. Both were of Italianate design and built at the same time in 1850. This was the home of Francis Dodge Jr., the first born son of Francis Dodge Sr. Unlike Robert Dodge, however, Francis lost his import-export business in 1857, and he lost this house to Henry Cooke. Francis Jr. and his family moved to 3052 P Street, a house within what is known as Cooke's Row, where he began a career with the government as the collector of customs for Georgetown.

Site F16: Stoddart Apartments at 2900 Q Street. Here stood a large house with long, side porches, according to Grace Ecker in her *A Portrait of Old Georgetown*. The home was owned by Gen. Henry Lockwood, whose son James accompanied Gen. Adolphus W. Greeley in his three-year exploration of the North Pole from 1881 to 1884. The expedition set a record for reaching the most northerly point at that time on May 13, 1882. However, Greeley lost 19 of his 25 party members, including James, when relief ships failed to appear. Greeley wrote about the expedition in his *Three Years of Arctic Service*, published in 1886, and he wrote about other Arctic adventures before his death in 1935.

SITE F17: DUMBARTON HOUSE AT 2715 Q STREET. Here is a significant mansion with a long history. Built in 1798 for Samuel Jackson, the house created a dead end on Q Street near Rock Creek Park. Joseph Nourse, a former aide-de-camp to Gen. Charles Lee during the Revolutionary War and, later, registrar of the U.S. Treasury from Washington to Andrew Jackson, bought the property in 1805. Nourse lived here until 1813 when he sold the house to Charles Carroll, a nephew of Daniel Carroll of Duddington, one of the early landowners of Washington, D.C. It is understood that Carroll named the house Bellevue.

DUMBARTON HOUSE. Among the last owners of the home was Sarah Whitall, related by marriage to the important Rittenhouse family. The Rittenhouses were direct descendants of William Rittenhouse, who produced the first paper in the United States in Pennsylvania about 1700. The Rittenhouses lived in the house until 1896. In 1915, Bellevue was physically moved from the middle of Q Street to its present site. Later, in 1928, the National Society of the Colonial Dames of America bought the property and renamed it Dumbarton House.

SITE F18: MOUNT ZION CEMETERY IN THE 2700 BLOCK OF Q STREET (BEHIND THE BUILDING).
Since 1809, when Ebenezer Eliason purchased this lot for use by the Montgomery Street Church,
it has served as a cemetery for slaves and members of the church where "50% of congregation
was colored bretheren [*sic*]." One of the vaults in the original cemetery was said to have been
used as a hiding place along the Underground Railroad, a series of secret places used to help
escaped slaves reach the northern states and Canada before and during the Civil War. Formed
in 1842, the Female Union Band Society bought adjacent land in 1879 for the burial of free
blacks, and, together, these two burial grounds formed the Mount Zion Cemetery. This area is
directly adjacent to Oak Hill Cemetery, the "whites only" burial ground in use before and after
the Civil War. In 1975, Mount Zion Cemetery was added to the National Register of Historic
Places and was saved from demolition—a fate not shared by the former Presbyterian Burial
Ground on Volta Place (Site D6).

SITE F19: DUMBARTON BRIDGE AT THE EAST END OF Q STREET. This bridge, over Rock Creek Park, was designed by Glenn Brown and his son Bedford in 1914 and is one of the few curved bridges in the United States. The bronze set of bison at each end of the bridge, designed by A. Phimister Proctor, add a unique character to the structure and are the reason why the bridge is sometimes referred to as the "Buffalo Bridge." Each buffalo is 7 feet high and just about actual size. Where once they roamed the midwest plains of the United States, they are only now returning in sufficient numbers to avoid extinction. Look above the arches and see if you can spot the bas relief Aztec Indian heads. These sandstone sculptures, 28 in all, were executed by Glenn Brown and placed along each of the curved arches on each side of the bridge. The center arch measures about 43 feet across, the longest of all five concrete arches. Down below is the Rock Creek Parkway. Cross the bridge and you are in the Embassy Row section of Washington, D.C., near Sheridan Circle and Massachusetts Avenue.

Site F20: Evermay at 1623 Twenty-eighth Street. The high brick wall surrounds one of the most enduring estates in Georgetown. It is an 18th-century Georgian manor house worthy of the name, and was built in 1792 by Samuel Davidson, an early speculator of land in the new Federal City who once owned the land where the White House is today. Lewis Grant, Davidson's nephew, inherited Evermay only after he changed his name to Davidson. The new Davidson's daughter Eliza married Charles Dodge in 1847, and so Evermay became another Dodge home. Evermay was almost razed for the building of a hotel in the 1920s but was saved through citizen action. Today, Evermay is still a private home.

Site F21: Mackall House at 1623 Twenty-ninth Street. The WPA Guide of 1937 says that the southern wing of this house was built about 1717, but that claim is probably disputed. Still, the house sits on the original land grant given to George Beall and known as the Rock of Dumbarton. George Beall sold the property to his daughter Christina Beall, who married Benjamin Mackall. Their son Louis inherited the property in 1839. Herman Hollerith, inventor of the tabulating machine (Site A36), lived here in the early 1900s. Other prominent people who have lived here include "Wild Bill" Donovan, the head of the original CIA, Philip Graham, the publisher of The *Washington Post*, and others. The Mackall House is still a private residence.

SITE F22: HURST HOME FOR THE BLIND AT 3050 R STREET. Founded in 1899 at 915 E Street NW, the Home for the Blind raised enough money by subscription and from the sale of its house in 1915 to purchase the lot and home of Brooke Williams (see below), the grandson of Brooke Beall. The house, an 18-room, Federal-style home built about 1835, was razed about 1915 to build the Home for the Blind. The home is named for Henry and Annie Hurst, who left an estate of $500,000. Brooke Beall inherited the house and land as part of his mother's estate. She had inherited it from her father, Brooke Beall, a distinguished relative of George Beall, one of the owners of Georgetown when it was incorporated in 1751, and Ninian Beall, the first patentee of the area that now includes Georgetown. His daughter Harriet married the Baron Bodisco, the Ambassador of Russia, in 1849. She was 16, and he was 63. It is just another incredible tale from one of the leading families of Georgetown.

BROOKE WILLIAMS HOME, C. 1900.

SITE F23: TUDOR PLACE AT 1644 THIRTY-FIRST STREET. Imagine that the central section of this structure did not exist and only the two wings on either side did. This shows how far Francis Loundes had gotten in 1794 towards completing this Federal-style mansion. In 1805, Martha Parke Custis, granddaughter of Martha Washington, bought the unfinished house and commissioned William Thornton, the architect of the U.S. Capitol and the White House, to redesign and finish the central portion. It is said that before the central section could be completed, the family lived in the east wing and watched the burning of Washington in 1814 from its windows. The house was finally completed in 1815, pretty much as it stands today.

SITE F24: COOKE ROW AT 3007–3029 Q STREET. Henry D. Cooke, the first governor of the District of Columbia and a brother to financier Jay Cooke, invested in real estate in the city. He bought this property and in 1868 built a series of impressive Victorian homes, except for the two "bookends" built in the Second Empire style. Dr. Walter Reed, the physician who helped cure yellow fever in 1900, lived in 3021. Walter Reed Hospital in Washington, D.C., is named for this medical pioneer.

SITE F25: BOWIE HOUSE AT 3124 Q STREET. Look up or you might just walk by this historic house. It is set rather high on a terrace overlooking Q Street. Washington Bowie, George Washington's godchild, built the center section of this two-story Georgian-style home in 1805. Bowie's descendants include the famous Col. James Bowie of the Alamo and Col. Bezin Bowie, inventor of the Bowie knife. During the War of 1812, the British drove Washington Bowie out of his shipping business and he lost everything, including this home. In 1890, John Sevier bought the property and remodeled the home so that it had a colonial look. It is now an Episcopal Church Home. The photo is *c.* 1900.

SITE F26: WISCONSIN AND Q STREETS. This photo, taken *c.* 1940s, shows what this corner looked like before the block was widened in 1949. Judging from the number of trees that were present at this time, many must have been lost to the construction.

SITE F27: WEST STREET PRESBYTERIAN CHURCH AT 3115 P STREET. When the parishioners planned to move from the Bridge Street Presbyterian Church because of commercial construction nearby along M Street (Site A1), they bought four vacant lots here in 1865. They commissioned architect James McGill to design a Gothic Revival–style chapel. A residence for the pastor was also built on this lot. By 1873, the congregation was ready to move, and a full-scale Gothic Revival church was built between the now-named Cissel Chapel and the residence. Gravesites were moved to the Presbyterian Burial Ground near Volta Place (Site D6), and the bricks from the original church were used in the construction of the new church. In 1918, the name of the church was changed to the Georgetown Presbyterian Church.

Stephen Bloomer Balch was founder and first pastor of the Bridge Street Presbyterian Church, predecessor to the West Street Presbyterian Church. Rev. Balch came to Georgetown in 1778 and preached at local churches and taught at Georgetown College. He founded the Bridge Street Church about 1780 and remained its pastor until his death on September 7, 1833. Grace Dunlop Ecker writes in *A Portrait of Old Georgetown* that "[e]very house in town was hung in black, all the stores and ? were closed and the bells tolled as his body was carried to the church." Dr. Balch was 87 years old.

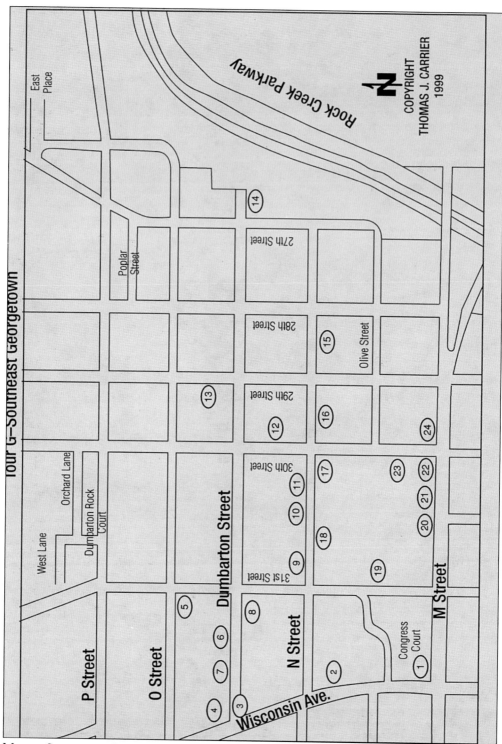

MAP OF SOUTHEAST GEORGETOWN.

Tour G

SOUTHEAST
GEORGETOWN

We are heading back toward the commercial main street of Georgetown once again. The large estates that are so prevalent on the northern hilltops of Georgetown have been replaced by the traditional townhouses, rowhouses, and tavern sites.

That is not to say that large, comfortable residences are uncommon here. In fact, this is probably the most historic sector of your walking tour. For instance, the large French-Kennedy House on N Street tells an early story of Georgetown history and also a modern one that includes the brief stay of the late Jacqueline Kennedy after the assassination of her husband, Pres. John F. Kennedy, in 1963.

The oldest building left in Washington, D.C., is located along M Street and called, appropriately enough, the Old Stone House. It was once thought that Suter's Tavern was located here. Suter's Tavern was an important historical site because the legislation creating the Federal City was signed by George Washington there. The story has since been discredited, and the Suter's Tavern location remains a mystery. Still, the Old Stone House provides a very refreshing look at life in Georgetown in the 18th century. The first survey point in 1751 was completed in the next block.

Col. Ninian Beall was said to have built the very first structure, a fishing lodge, on Thirtieth Street. Naturally, it is long gone, but its site still provides history of a different sort—the first female recipient of the Medal of Honor lived there.

Since this is your last tour, I hope you enjoyed learning about the history of Georgetown. There is really so much more history than can be accommodated here. That is Georgetown today as it was yesterday.

Site G1: Linthicum Hardware Store on the Northeast Corner of Wisconsin and M Streets (Riggs Bank). Edward M. Linthicum had his hardware store at this site in the early 1800s. He resided at 3019 P Street (Site F5) until he bought Dumbarton Oaks in 1846 (Site E1). This photo shows the corner in the late 19th century with a streetcar passing south to K Street. Here, General Edward Braddock with his young aide, Col. George Washington, passed by on their march to Fort Duquesne during the French and Indian Wars in 1755. When Braddock was killed on this expedition, Col. George Washington led the army to safety.

Site G2: John Lutz Home at 1255 Wisconsin Avenue. John Lutz bought the present home, the Aged Woman's Home, in 1804 to manage his father's leather goods store. During the Revolutionary War, Lutz headed General Washington's personal guard detail. His grandson, a theatre producer, introduced him to his bride, Laura Keene, whose performance during *Our American Cousin* was interrupted by the assassination of Abraham Lincoln on April 14, 1865. Her cuff helped staunch the flow of blood from Lincoln's head wound. Visit Ford's Theatre and the historic exhibit in its basement for a more complete story.

SITE G3: MONTGOMERY TAVERN SITE (AU PIED DE COCHON RESTAURANT) AT 1363 WISCONSIN AVENUE. On this site stood the rambling old Montgomery Tavern, which had enough stables to house 300 teams of horses (yes, 300!). A large inn, it served as the auction house for tobacco and other produce. No other information is available about when it operated or when it disappeared. By the way, Victor Yevchenko defected to the United States from the Soviet Union from this restaurant on November 2, 1985. Find the brass plate at the table where he sat.

SITE G4: DUMBARTON THEATER AT 1351 WISCONSIN AVENUE. The Dumbarton Theatre was one of the first motion picture theatres in Washington when it was built in 1913. The building was a converted 1880 commercial structure. Its curvilinear facade, arches, and rounded Italianate windows have long since been hidden under modern "stone." The Georgetown movie theatre opened in 1950 but closed sometime in the 1980s. It is now a jewelry outlet store.

SITE G5: CHRIST EPISCOPAL CHURCH ON THIRTY-FIRST AND O STREETS. With its tall, red-brick tower, this imposing church was built in 1885 from a design by Henry Laws. In the 1890s, this church became the spiritual home for the exclusive, old-line families, known as the Georgetown Assembly, who were notably southern sympathizers during the Civil War. Organized about 1810, the assembly of early families of society gathered to dance and socialize at various locations around Washington, including Forrest Hall (Site B21). Here, their children took religious instruction at Sunday school, married, and, at times, were even buried.

SITE G6: MCKENNY HOUSE AT 3123 DUMBARTON AVENUE. Henry Foxall, a munitions manufacturer, gave this house to his daughter Mary Ann and her new husband, Samuel McKenny, as a wedding gift in 1818. In *A Portrait of Old Georgetown*, Grace Ecker notes that the family still lived in the house as of 1950.

SITE G7: DUMBARTON METHODIST EPISCOPAL CHURCH AT 3127 DUMBARTON AVENUE. The information on this church comes from a small walking tour guide printed in 1971, which says that the church was built in 1849, but the facade was added in 1898. During the Civil War, the building was a Union hospital where the poet, Walt Whitman, served as a male nurse. The church was also frequented by Abraham Lincoln where, on March 7, 1863, he was observed crying during a service by a reporter from The *Evening Star*.

SITE G8: BILLINGS SCHOOL AT 3100–3108 DUMBARTON AVENUE. This school was named for Mary Billings, who opened a school for children, both white and black, in 1807. Because of the lack of racial division, the first school was forced to close, but Billings opened this school in 1810 where she taught African-American children exclusively until her death in 1826. A school for boys operated here for a time, but not much more is known about the building after that.

SITE G9: WHEATLEY ROW AT 3041–3045 N STREET. Wealthy lumber merchant Francis Wheatley built these five rowhouses between 1850 and 1860. These are great townhomes that feature Victorian embellishments including long, narrow windows.

SITE G10: THE BEALL MANSION AT 3033 N STREET. The central portion of this structure is said to have been built with the money George Beall received after selling part of the Rock of Dunbarton for the establishment of the Town of George (now Georgetown) in 1751. It is considered to be the oldest brick edifice in Georgetown, dating from 1780. This house originally stood across the street at 3032 N Street. When the Town of George was created, this house stood within the northern boundary, and because this property was sold to create the town, the house had to be moved or demolished. So, it was moved. Thomas Beall inherited the property in 1780 but exchanged it for other properties owned by his brother George Jr. It was during this exchange that the original spelling of Dunbarton was inadvertently changed to Dumbarton, the current spelling.

SITE G11: THE FRENCH-JACQUELINE KENNEDY HOUSE AT 3017 N STREET. Though it is difficult to see in this photo, this massive brick house, built in 1794–1796 by Thomas Beall, was an investment property, as many homes were in Georgetown. Maj. George Peter, who organized the famous "Flying Artillery" during the War of 1812, was one of the famous names of the period who rented the home. The house was first named for Col. William E.P. French, a cousin of Daniel Chester French, the sculptor of the Lincoln Memorial. Secretary of War Newton D. Baker lived here during World War I, and, most recently, Jacqueline Kennedy moved here from the White House in 1963 and stayed approximately one year, later moving overseas to escape the constant public attention.

JACQUELINE KENNEDY ONASSIS, C. **1961.** While overseas, she married multi-millionaire shipping tycoon Aristotle Onassis, in Greece in 1968, where she lived until his death in 1975. Later, Mrs. Onassis moved to New York and began a career as a book editor for Random House until her death in 1993. Visit a small stone memorial to Mrs. Onassis near Decatur House in D.C. recognizing her work in preserving the 19th-century charm of Lafayette Square across from the White House.

SITE G12: COLONIAL APARTMENTS AT 1305–1311 THIRTIETH STREET. While the building itself has its own curious history, the lot was originally the site of Ninian Beall's hunting lodge, the first building erected on his newly granted Rock of Dunbarton in 1703. The current building was erected in the mid-1800s as Miss Lydia English's Seminary for young ladies. During the Civil War, the building served as a hospital where Dr. Mary Walker Edwards, a surgeon, tended Union soldiers and became the only woman to be awarded the Medal of Honor.

SITE G13: MOUNT ZION UNITED METHODIST CHURCH AT 1334 TWENTY-NINTH STREET. The oldest of the African-American churches in Georgetown is here. Organized in 1816 on land purchased from Henry Foxall, Mt. Zion Church had one of the first schools dedicated to teaching African-American children and was, in addition, a way station, like its cemetery farther north, on the Underground Railroad. Alfred Pope contributed the land for the current church, the construction was completed by church members, and the building was dedicated in 1884.

SITE G14 BAPTIST CHURCH AT TWENTY-SEVENTH AND DUMBARTON AVENUE. This is the earliest known Baptist Church in Georgetown and was founded by the Reverend Sandy Alexander in 1862. Previously, the congregation met in a smaller building at Twenty-first and O Streets. The current structure was consecrated in 1882.

SITE G15: DECATUR HOUSE AT 2812 N STREET. If you have been following the tours up to now, you will have read about the persistence of some historical "facts" even when they may not be true (Site F2). Here is another example. After her husband, the famed Commodore Stephen Decatur, was killed in a duel at Bladensburg, Maryland, in 1820 by another naval officer, Susan Decatur was to have moved to Georgetown from her house on Lafayette Square. Rumors persist that this is the house to which she moved. This Federal-style house was either built in 1816 or 1799, depending on which resource is consulted. The architect was John Stull Williams.

SITE G16: FOXALL HOUSE AT 2908 N STREET. Built in 1820, this is certainly a smaller house, or at least it seems that way with its small windows and smaller door. Henry Foxall made his fortune as the manufacturer of reliable weapons that were of particular importance during the War of 1812. Foxall, a Wesleyan lay minister, reconciled his dual roles this way, "If I do make guns to destroy men's bodies, I build churches to save their souls." Foxall built several churches in Washington and was also, briefly, the mayor of the city. He died in 1823 while on a visit to England.

HENRY FOXALL. Foxall was born in 1760 in England but immigrated to Dublin where he learned his trade in the iron foundries. Later, he took his craft to Philadelphia and in 1794 became a partner with Robert Morris, the greatest financier of his time and signer of the Declaration of Independence. By 1799, Foxall had moved to Georgetown and opened his own foundry supplying weapons to the government during the War of 1812 with England. A convert to Methodism, Foxall financed many churches in Washington, D.C., and Georgetown throughout his life.

Site G17: Dunlop-Lincoln House at 3014 N Street.

John Laird moved here in 1800 after briefly living at 3017 N Street (Site G14) while waiting for this house to be built. The home was inherited by Laird's son-in-law, who was removed as chief justice of the District of Columbia Circuit Court by President Lincoln because of his Southern sympathies. Interestingly, Lincoln's son Robert Todd Lincoln, the former secretary of War and ambassador to Great Britain, bought the house in 1915 and lived there until his death in 1926. At one time, the only remaining boundary stone of the Town of George was located in the garden. However, the site was divided into two estates, and the stone is now in the garden of 1248 Thirtieth Street, a former carriage house just around the corner. It is a private, walled compound and not open to the public.

Site G18: The Riggs-Riley House at 3038 N Street.

Romulus Riggs purchased this great Federal home as a wedding present for his new wife in 1812. Romulus was a prominent member of the Riggs family, the founders of Riggs National Bank.

SITE G19: CUSTOM HOUSE AT 1215 THIRTY-FIRST STREET. Architect Ammi Young, the supervising architect of the U.S. Treasury, produced governmental-use buildings such as this Italianate-style Georgetown Custom House in 1857. With Georgetown as a main shipping port, it is only natural that it would have its own customs house. Today, the building is the Georgetown branch of the U.S. Postal Service.

SITE G20: THE OLD STONE HOUSE AT 3051 M STREET. The Old Stone House is believed to be the oldest surviving pre-Revolutionary building in Washington. Set on Original Lot #3 in 1751, the present structure was built as a house and carpenter shop in 1765 by Christopher Layman. After just finishing the house, Mr. Layman died. His widow, Rachel, sold the house and lot to Cassandra Chew, who added the back wing in 1767, and the home remained in her family for nearly 100 years. The National Park Service bought the property in 1950 and renovated it to correspond to Layman's inventory. It was open to the public in 1960. *Open Wednesday-Sunday, 10 a.m. to 4 p.m. Admission is free.*

SITE G21: LOUGHBOROUGH-PATTERSON HOUSE AT 3039–41 M STREET. Built c. 1801–1806, this is the city home of Nathan Loughborough, a town magistrate who brought suit against the U.S. government for charging taxes on his townhouse on the grounds that it constituted "taxation without representation." Loughborough's feud with Thomas Jefferson, that "Little Red Breeches," is legend. This was at one time the office of the D.C. chapter of the Junior League.

SITE G22: THOMAS SIM LEE CORNER ON THIRTIETH AND M STREETS. This was the home of former governor of Maryland Thomas Sim Lee. He was an officer in the Maryland militia and a member of the early Provisional Assembly that wrote the constitution of Maryland. Lee was instrumental in providing logistical support for his friend, Gen. George Washington, during the American Revolution. The house was saved from demolition by Georgetown residents in 1951. Here is the Initial Survey Point of 1752, marking the eastern boundary of the original Town of George in 1752. Beyond this was the Rock Creek and undeveloped forest.

125

SITE G23: FLEET HOUSE AT 1208 THIRTIETH STREET. Dr. James Fleet moved to this house in 1843 and opened a school for African-American students the same year. Fleet earned his medical degree through the sponsorship of the American Colonization Society. The society's aim was to return freed slaves to Liberia, Africa. However, Fleet refused to go, and the society withdrew their support. He spent his career teaching music and administering his school, rather than practicing medicine. The *Guide to Black Washington* does not record what happened to Dr. Fleet later in life.

SITE G24: THE UNION TAVERN, AT NE CORNER OF M AND THIRTIETH STREETS. Begun as a speculative development through public subscription, the tavern was meant to attract new visitors to the Federal City when it was built in 1796. In 1800, John Suter, already the owner of the Fountain Inn, or Suter's Tavern (Sites A26 and A37), bought it at auction. Pres. George Washington attended his last public function here on February 22, 1799 (he died in December that year), and many national and international notables of the age such as the 18th-century French statesman Talleyrand, the Bonapartes, and others were guests here. The tavern remained here until the 1940s when it was finally razed.

Selective Bibliography

American Institute of Architects, *AIA Guide to the Architecture of Washington, D.C.*, Johns Hopkins University Press, 1994.

American Guide Series, *Washington: City and Capital*, Federal Writers' Project, Works Progress Administration, Government Printing Office, 1937.

Arnebeck, Bob, *Through a Fiery Trial: Building Washington 1790–1800*, Madison Books, 1991.

Brown, George Rothwell, *Washington: A Not Too Serious History*, Norman Publishing, Co., 1930.

Caemmerer, H.P., *Washington: The National Capitol*, US Government Printing Office, 1932.

Delany, Kevin, *A Walk Through Georgetown*, Kevin Delany Publications, 1971.

Ecker, Grace Dunlop, *A Portrait of Old George Town*, The Dietz Press, Inc., 1951.

Fitzpatrick, Sandra, Goodwin, Maria R., *The Guide to Black Washington*, Hippocrene Books, Inc., 1993.

Georgetown Architecture: The Waterfront, Historic American Buildings Survey #4, National Park Service and US Commission of Fine Arts, 1968.

Georgetown Historic Waterfront, National Park Service and US Commission of Fine Arts, 1968.

Hines, Christian, *Early Recollections of Washington City*, Junior League, reprint 1981.

Historic Georgetown, Inc., *A Walking Guide to Historic Georgetown*, reprint 1980.

Mackall, S. Somervell, *Early Days of Washington*, no publisher listed, 1899.

McClelland, Nancy, *Georgetown Houses of the Federal Period*, Architectural Book Publishing, Co., 1949.

Mitchell, Mary, *Chronicles of Georgetown Life: 1865–1900*, Seven Locks Press, 1986.

Rose, C.B., *Arlington County, Virginia: A History*, Arlington Historical Society, 1976.

Photo Credits

All images are courtesy of the Washingtoniana Division, D.C. Public Library (including those from The *Washington Post*), except for the following: courtesy of the ARCHITECT OF THE U.S. CAPITOL: B20; courtesy of the BOOKHOUSE: page 4, Sites A1, A53, B8, B10, C1, page 62, C2, C5, D3, D11, D12, E1, E7, F17, F20, F22, F25, G6, G14, G16; courtesy of ALBERT EISENBERG: Site B20; courtesy of GEORGETOWN UNIVERSITY LIBRARY: Site C1 (photo of Bishop Carroll), D2; courtesy of the collection of the HISTORICAL SOCIETY OF WASHINGTON, D.C.: A49, A54; courtesy of the NATIONAL PARK SERVICE: page 8, 9, Sites A3, A4, A5, A6, A8, A9, A10, A11, A12, A23, A25, A31, A32, A35, A39, A40, A41, A44, A45, A48, B17; courtesy of THE WASHINGTON POST: Site A7 (photo of William O. Douglas), A51, D11 (photo of "Duke" Ellington), G11 (photo of Jackie Kennedy Onassis); courtesy of the collection of ROBERT A. TRUAX: Sites G1, G4; courtesy of THE AUTHOR: A7, A9, A13, A14, A15, A17, A18, A19, A20, A22, A26, A34, A36, A37, A42, A43, A44, A50, A52, A55, B1, B2, B4, B6, B7, B9, B11, B13, B15, B16, B19, B21, D1, D4, D5, D8, D9, D10, D11, D13, D15 E8, E10, E12, F1, F2, F3, F4, F5, F6, F7, F8, F11, F12, F13, F14, F15, F18, F19, F22, F24, F27, G2, G3, G5, G8, G9, G10, G11 (photo of home), G12, G13, G14, G17, G18, G19, G21, G22, G23.

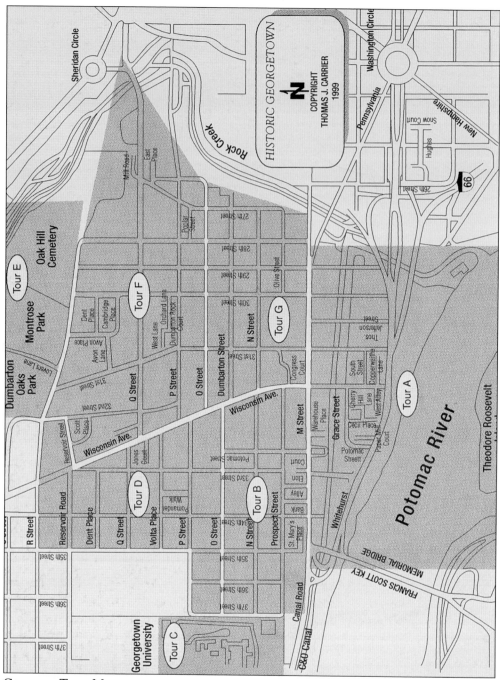

COMPLETE TOUR MAP.